To my mum
Like a snowdrop in mid-winter, you pushed
through cold environments to flourish and
grow and I am immensely proud of you. I know
you haven't heard those words enough in your
lifetime but I hope this book acknowledges
your steadfastness to raising your bar.

To my only daughter
Because we fail, we learn and
grow. Love conquers all.

To my boys
Ryan and Kane: Be good men because you have
been wonderful boys 90 per cent of the time.
Troy: You have given me wings to fly
and see life with a new perspective.

Denise Lewis DBE is a retired Team GB track and field athlete who specialised in the heptathlon. She won the gold medal in the heptathlon at the 2000 Sydney Olympics and bronze at the 1996 Atlanta Olympics. Lewis is considered to be one of the 'golden girls' of British athletics, having been inducted into the UK Athletics Hall of Fame in 2011, and has twice been runner-up in BBC's Sports Personality of the Year Awards, in 1998 and 2000. Since retiring from athletics, she has become one of the nation's most popular broadcasters and sports pundits, as well as lighting up our screens on *Strictly Come Dancing* and, most recently, *The Masked Dancer*.

ADAPT-ABILITY

DENISE LEWIS

PIATKUS

PIATKUS

First published in Great Britain in 2025 by Piatkus

1 3 5 7 9 10 8 6 4 2

Edited by Sarah Ivens

A CIP catalogue record for this book
is available from the British Library.

HBK: 978-0-349-44187-0
TPB: 978-0-349-44188-7

Typeset in Garamond by M Rules
Printed and bound in Great Britain by
Clays Ltd, Elcograf S.p.A

Papers used by Piatkus are from well-managed forests
and other responsible sources.

Piatkus
An imprint of
Little, Brown Book Group
Carmelite House
50 Victoria Embankment
London EC4Y 0DZ

The authorised representative
in the EEA is
Hachette Ireland
8 Castlecourt Centre
Dublin 15, D15 XTP3, Ireland
(email: info@hbgi.ie)

An Hachette UK Company
www.hachette.co.uk

www.littlebrown.co.uk

Contents

Introduction

I can't remember a time when I didn't have an inner determination to succeed. As a child, in the playground, I would set up races and a scoring system so that the fastest girl in the school (me) would have to compete with the fastest boy. I loved the playfulness of it, the camaraderie in my team of girls but, if I'm totally honest, I also loved the thrill of the competition. I wanted to prove myself. I wanted to be challenged. And, since childhood, in that area of my life – athletics – I knew I could win. I worked hard in my other school subjects too until, in my early teens, while writing an essay in my English class, I got a clear vision of what I wanted to do with my life: to compete in the Olympics. From that moment on, getting a medal became my only goal, and soon I was utterly focused on making it come true. Every other aspect of my life was honed down or pushed to one side to make my dream a reality. Much like the portrait mode on an iPhone, the Olympics were the main part of the image, and everything else blurred away around the edges.

Now, in my fifties, success looks different. *I* look different. I'm a mother of four children, a wife, I've continued to commit to a career as a sports pundit, I'm a former president of Commonwealth Games England and an author. As women get older, there is sometimes a sense that they should retire from public life and stand to one side, or that it might be more appropriate for them to be less visible in some way. You may have felt that way at work or in social situations: pushed aside, or told you were past your prime. Well, I'm here to say: no way – you are not! You are just at a point of pivot, of change, of adapting to new circumstances and commitments. Indeed, women need to do this at every age and stage of their life: when they marry, become a mother, become the boss, or take on the role of mothering their mother. If anything, a woman's ability to adapt makes us more valuable, not less. Often, we just need society and those around us to adapt to change as well as we do.

I'm fighting the stereotype by continuing to step out – and to step up – in both my personal and work life. From the outside, it might have looked as if I had reached my highest power when I was competing around the world and winning gold at the Olympics, and in some ways I did feel incredibly powerful back then. But, in reality, it's only in the past decade that I've truly stepped into my power – and I've done it by being adaptable.

What people know about my career is only one small part of my life; it is not the full picture. I've been told that from the outside it looks as if I have a charmed life, and in some ways I do: I have my family, my friends, my good health – and I am appreciative of those things – but many of the external things for which I am considered lucky haven't come about through luck at all. I have them because I've worked hard to create what I have for myself and my family by being resilient, conscientious and adaptable when I've run into hurdles and setbacks. Alongside my successful sporting and presenting careers, I've had to overcome obstacles linked to my roots, from my childhood and from the decisions I've made.

My own evolution has shown that you really can achieve great things even when the odds are stacked against you. As a child, I had a huge amount of independence – too much, some might think – and very little money, because my mum was raising me on her own, working day and night to support us both. As a shy teenager, I felt quite lost at times, trying to work out my place alongside peers and trying to fit in while harbouring a dream to become an athletics champion. As a woman of colour, I have often been the minority in the room in terms of ethnicity *and* gender, but instead of cowering away, I strode out into any room and did what I had to do, masking my fears and doubts as best as I could.

From conversations I've had with many women over the years, I know that every time I use *my* inner strength to put myself forward, I'm showing others that they can do this, too. And now, finally, as a woman who truly knows herself, I feel able to share my lessons and beliefs with others. In this book, I'm going to walk you through the thought processes and good habits I have found and adapted to be able to not just feel *welcome* in any room but to *own* it, to stand on stage and present to an audience with confidence. In the following chapters, I hope to prove to all of you that whatever life throws at you, and wherever you have come from, if you set your intention on something, you can absolutely achieve it. Yes, you will face barriers, we all do, but rather than seeing a difficulty as the end of the track, see it as a hurdle to leap over, a challenge to grow from, a chance to grow.

Stories from my journey as an athlete are woven throughout the book, because they demonstrate how mental agility can be rehearsed, practised and, most importantly, taught. Through repetition and regular reflection, the athlete improves their performance. Likewise, *people* can improve – in terms of both their home lives and work. It requires daily mental engagement and looking at the granular details of what needs to be done to move forward in a positive way. During those 'make or break' moments in athletics, which have the potential to feel incredibly stressful, you must control the fight-or-flight reaction of your nervous system by staying in a ventral vagal (calm, collected) state. How do you do this? Just like a heptathlon, by using mindset tools, which I'll be teaching you here. I will be sharing with you the seven skills I have lived by to become my best self, all the tools, processes and ideas I have uncovered across the decades that can help us to face whatever life throws at us with self-belief, strength and the ability to stand our ground. You can handle the ups and downs of life, I promise. Life will not always be perfect, life will not always be easy, but you can adapt to the lows and cherish the highs when you accept that you need to put some work in – and you learn to accept yourself.

My journey through world-class sport, from playground to gold medal for the heptathlon, has taught me a great deal about my personal character but also about what we *all* need to embrace to get the best out of ourselves. Hurdler. Jumper. Thrower. Sprinter. Woman. Mother. Athlete. Friend. Colleague. Daughter. The mastery of multiple disciplines is a gold thread that has dictated my success both on and off the track field. Since retiring from athletics, the importance of adaptability, and the lessons that derive from it, drive the coping strategies that I implement not only as a working mum of four children, but also in all the other roles I play. The tools I developed in my career are still those I reach for. They underpin my ability to juggle multiple competing demands, to recognise how to draw from different sources of strength, and they allow me to become different versions of myself depending on who needs me, or – most importantly sometimes – what I need.

Being adaptable is important, because without it you can remain stuck – physically or mentally – in a situation that doesn't serve you; you can revolve in a cycle of old thinking that doesn't push you forward. For me, adaptability has been the key to stepping up into my power, and I believe it will help you to step into yours, too. In the following chapters, I will encourage you to:

1. **Maintain your identity** Be prepared to adjust. Learn from your early years and know that life is full of unforeseeable events, both good and bad. This book will show you how to handle change without falling apart.

2. **Build resilience** In this chapter I explain how winning takes work, whether in sports, our career or in our marriage and family, and we can also guide our children

towards independence by building resilience in them. Difficult experiences from our past give us an opportunity to learn and aim to improve our approach for future progress. In a challenging situation happening right now, when we focus on the present, rather than the past or future, we can boost our pathway towards achieving our goal.

3. **Plan for success** Visualise your success and believe in yourself and your plan for success. This chapter encourages you to visualise your trajectory and know that when others believe in you, your belief in yourself strengthens and spurs you forward to achieve more. Plan and work out how family and career life can work together and at which point it is best for you to combine both. Be adaptable but with a defined plan in mind. Remember your core values; they will help you to stay on course for your ultimate goal.

4. **Follow your instincts** Our natural instincts are very strong, and we ignore them at our peril as we go through life. This chapter explains how to use your instincts to make big and small life decisions, whether in your career or as a mother. When you believe in yourself, your self-empowerment will grow as you nurture the skills of adaptability that are the core of this book.

Visualisation or meditation can help you to follow and benefit from your instincts.

5. **Own your space** When embracing adaptability, you might find that your friendships or acquaintances change in pace with your new interests, priorities and passions. Approach your life positively and avoid comparing yourself to the people around you, because everyone (and every family) is different. Stay focused on your own path and benefit from the validation of others who truly appreciate what you have achieved.

6. **Let go and seek support** You need some downtime, but in our busy lives today we can become overwhelmed with the demands of career/work, family needs and maintaining a (reasonably) organised home. This chapter asks that you find different ways to ensure that your relationship with your spouse or partner can thrive with understanding and that everyone in the family recognises why their help in running the home is also essential.

7. **Find inner strength and peace** You can become tense and irritable when fatigued, and bad reactions to these stresses can then creep in. These are signs that you are not making time for yourself, but you can, and should,

change this. This chapter isolates the possible stressors and, more importantly, suggests methods for finding composure and calm to help change your reactions during those moments that annoy you. The emphasis here is on you being able to be peaceful in your own space and to deal with the stresses of life in a considered way.

To stay sane throughout our busy lives, we will need to compartmentalise and move on. I recognised a long time ago this need to be able to flick a mental switch to regain focus and to transition from one challenge to the next. The ability to stay on task without the mind drifting to the things you should have done or didn't do well enough is difficult. I used to mentally struggle in the transitions between certain heptathlon disciplines – particularly between the first and second events, 100-metre hurdles and the high jump. It's the shortest of all the breaks between the events, and therefore the shortest time to mentally get over any emotions you might be carrying.

When asked by my sports psychologist at the time how I could lose the emotional baggage so that it wouldn't impact my next event, I didn't have a clue. We talked about mental exercises and the use of visualisation, none of which worked for me initially. I would later learn to love and utilise these tools effectively, but right then I needed something else. A brilliant sports psychologist I was working with at the time around my first Olympics called Alma Thomas suggested that I try something physical to help me put my emotions into a black box and move on, and I remember telling her that I had seven different pairs of shoes for each event in the heptathlon – could that be something we could use? She thought that was a great idea, and so changing my shoes for each event became my trigger to dump the emotion, whether good or bad, and just to look forward. With time I got better and more practised at packaging up my emotions generally, but also by physically changing shoes and sending feelings off on a conveyor belt with a view to collecting the emotions again at a time when I could constructively evaluate them, allowed me to focus on what was needed in any particular moment. I'm not suggesting that you swap shoes every time you hit a mental roadblock, or you have to concentrate on one thing when another is stressing you out, but I can tell you about all the different mental and physical ways we have at our fingertips (or feet, perhaps) to help us adapt to a new situation quickly and successfully. (I describe this method in Chapter 2.)

Ultimately, what distinguishes high-level sport from the everyday is mindset. Unlocking the power of the mind, using it to push through pain and discomfort, taming the negative chatter and the repetition of good habits – *that* gets you to gold, on the track and in life. The life of an athlete has a clear purpose with a strategy, target-setting, self-motivation and adaptation, by applying a 'How can I be better today?' attitude. And this is a mindset that we can all work towards, whether in sports or in other parts of our lives.

In fact, since retiring from athletics, I've found myself using the same tools that helped me to succeed in my sporting career within motherhood. In the seven events of a heptathlon, you must be able to razor-focus on the event that you're about to compete in and then, as soon as it's done, transition to the next. There's no time to reflect or regret; you must keep moving forward. Raising four children, two of whom are neurodivergent, while continuing to grow my career has meant that in the same way that I needed to shift my focus from the 100-metre hurdles to the high jump, from the shot-put to the 200-metre race, I now have to adjust my mindset to adapt to work–life demands. As an athlete, I needed to stay calm and focused, even if I felt I had messed up an event, and as a mother I do, too. I don't always manage this, sometimes I lose my patience, but now when I'm on the edge of burnout, I find the support I need to ground myself. In this book, I will hand you the tools to be able to do the same. In each chapter, you will find prompt questions that will help you journal your own thoughts, feelings and successes. Base your answers to these on the examples in your own life and how you can make the tools in this book work for you so that you can become more adaptable.

It doesn't matter whether you're competing in the Olympic stadium, giving a keynote presentation, deciding whether or not to have children and then deciding if you should go back to work after becoming a mother, or you're having a job interview or negotiating bedtime with your toddler, there will be moments when your heart rate increases and you will feel out of control. The ability to zoom out and anchor yourself again so that you can meet the challenge in front of you straight on is a lifeline that can be taught and practised.

This book will also serve as a reminder to you that sometimes it's not you who needs to adapt, but your surroundings and the people in your orbit. I understand the competing demands that are placed upon women, the impossible expectations where we are presumed to be strong and capable enough to care for everyone, while being malleable and reticent to put ourselves first or to ask for what we deserve. In reading my seven lessons for success, you will be able to unlock your most adaptable self, while demanding the respect and courtesy from others to do the same. The world is changing; we *all* need to adapt to it – not just women. I will encourage you to embrace every part of your multifaceted identity as it changes, brave enough to stand out and stand up for yourself as it does.

I want to teach you that you can be your own world-class coach. I want to teach you the tools I have used in my career to build adaptability and resilience. And I want to teach you how to claim your space in this world proudly. I will share the seven lessons with you so that you can see how I've learned to be adaptable, and how much better your life will be with that ability.

Denise

CHAPTER 1

Maintain Your Identity

An identity would seem to be arrived at by the way in which the person faces and uses his experience.

JAMES BALDWIN,
WRITER AND CIVIL-RIGHTS ACTIVIST

Women are multifaceted: they are many things to many people, most of the time. This feeds into our identity, or identities: as a career woman, as well as mother; primary caregiver to ageing parents, as well as stay-at-home parent to toddlers; a social butterfly, who feels replenished spending time alone. Over the years, I've discovered many identities within myself, and I hold them all close to my heart. They are all integral parts of me, making me the person I am. As a mother, I go all in, and as a career woman, I do too. One doesn't need to erase the other; they can co-exist. I also hold my female friends very close and identify myself as a 'woman's woman'. Our identity can and should evolve over time, shedding parts of our past that no longer serve us as we add new layers that do. Yes, women are multifaceted, constantly evolving wonders.

Our first role is the one we were born into: as part of a family with an ancestral past. To better understand how we came to be the person we are now, we need to understand what went before. The struggles of our parents, grandparents, great-grandparents, and so on, might be passed down the generations (this is the basis of 'generational trauma') but so, too, will the triumphs and learning. When we understand the plight of those who came before us, we can learn how to adapt and improve on our own lives. I watched my mother do this – she decided that she would create a new path for herself and for me – and I have gone on to do the same for myself and my own children: always observing, reflecting, learning and *adapting*.

My heritage is a combination of Caribbean, South-East Asian, and African, and I was raised in England, in the Midlands, so there's a melting pot of cultural influences that all contribute towards who I am today. Some of the influences feel positive, whereas others can feel negative. There is the weight of expectation when you come from an immigrant family, as I do. I felt that there was pressure to secure my place in the world, and yet there were barriers in my way, as a black woman. Part of my identity, then, was developed within these parameters, but I decided to prove myself through athletics, and I took a running leap right over those barriers. I wasn't going to be held back; I was determined to keep rising. I still am.

STEP INTO THE LIFE THAT YOU CHOOSE FOR YOURSELF

Although we bring our heritage forward with us, we can also decide who we are as individuals. My identity draws on the music I love, and the spicy foods that I eat. I like style, fashion, being colourful and playful, make-up, dressing-up and feeling glamorous. I had a necklace designed for me by Annoushka Ducas featuring seven charms, each one based on how I view myself and my life and what was important to me: the treble clef for my love of music; the Olympic rings; a design representing the heptathlon; an afro comb to highlight my identity as a black woman; a seashell to represent my love of the ocean and Jamaica; and the clasping hands of women, to show

how we can and should support each other. The remaining charm is a figure of a woman with two suspended baskets of pearls – one in the left hand and one in the right. The pearls on the right are a representation of my children and family, the pearls on the left represent my work in its many forms. This is how I see myself: a woman trying to balance it all. Aren't we all? These are the scales of life, they're never constant – sometimes we give more to one role than another, constantly tilting and adapting to what is needed, what feels heavier. As long as you know what is important, you'll always come back to the centre. I love writing lists, because they help me physically to see what needs to be done, and I can order everything in priority. There is always one thing that is more pressing than another, despite other people trying to make their priorities yours. Adaptability is very much about adapting your way of thinking, therefore being present in the moment and reclaiming your time to be more efficient for you in the many roles that you have to fulfil.

As a mother, I'm a protector and a problem-solver: I lift, love, inspire, support, nurture and instil values. At work, I'm a team player and a forward-thinker. I bring my whole self to my job as a presenter: I add fun, but I'm also vulnerable and supportive, because I feel safe and confident to do so. Can you see how many layers there are to my identity, now? It will likely be the same for you.

EMBRACE YOUR IDENTITY

It might be important for you to understand how others view you and what their expectations of you might be; for example, we might be judged on our race, gender, ability or class, or where we're from, our education, and much more. Knowing that people will likely make snap judgements, and what that judgement might be, enables us to challenge preconceived ideas about who we are. Because, although we bring our heritage forward with us, we also decide who we are as individuals. We step into the life that we choose for ourselves.

Of course, it's not just about other people's view of you, it's also about knowing your own personality – which is part-genetic, part-environmental – and why you behave the way you do. The way you were raised will have an impact on how you view yourself and treat others. When you become intimately engaged with these details about who you are, how you function best and what you need in terms of support – you can operate at your optimum level.

One interesting question to ask yourself when thinking about identity, is this: who are you outside your career? We often jump straight into talking about our (paid) work when asked about ourselves, and it's a perfectly fine question – after all, we tend to spend many hours of our lives doing our job. But we need to remember that we are so much beyond this – so who are you? Where do you come from? What was your upbringing like? What does your life look like now? Who are you surrounded by? How does that feel? And, importantly: who do you *want* to be?

It's crucial that we understand ourselves well, so that we can show up in the world – at home, at work and in our relationships – with a really good understanding of both our past and present; our strengths and weaknesses. There's sometimes a temptation to brush a tricky past under the rug, but it doesn't disappear there, it grows. Instead, pull the rug back and explore those past challenges so that you can move forward feeling lighter. The sooner you've worked through your past and have become clear on where you'd like to be, how you'd like to operate and who you'd like to be around, the sooner you can start putting in place the actions that will complement this vision.

IT'S NEVER TOO LATE TO ADAPT

If you were to create a representation of yourself, what would it look like? Who are you? Ask yourself whether that's the 'you' that other people see, or the 'you' that you feel you are inside? Would you like to change how others see you, or how you see yourself? Because if you would, you are allowed to do so – and I encourage you to do this whenever you feel the pull. There is no age limit. This is about giving yourself permission to adapt and evolve your identity continually as you travel through life.

When I think about adapting as we get older, I think about my lovely mum: she is living proof that you're never too past it or stuck in the past to adapt your life for its betterment. For a long time, she was reluctant to change, because the buried trauma of two huge adjustments she'd had to make when she was younger (moving from Jamaica to the UK when she was eleven years old, then becoming a single mum in her late teens) were holding her back; she was frightened of fresh risks. But in the last few years, she's started to make small changes and reaped the rewards: she's taken up golf and found a whole new bunch of friends through that, and she is becoming more adventurous. I can see the sense of power and freedom it gives her – and that we all get when we make positive adaptations to our lives.

Sometimes what feels like fear or anxiety can actually be recalibrated as excitement. Nervous energy can feel overwhelming before a change – or just at the thought of it – especially if we've been living the same life for a long time, but it is this energy that gets us through the hard work of making that change. My mum is finally saying yes to more, which has been a long time coming, I think, due to her lack of belonging and self-advocacy. Now, to see her edging towards her seventieth birthday as a bit of a go-getter not only makes me proud but it also fills me with relief. She sees now, as I have since I was very young, that making tweaks and adjustments to your life is always good. It keeps us thinking, it keeps us active. Even if you realise a certain shift was wrong and you switch back to your old position, you'll have learned valuable life lessons and skills. Our environment does not stay the same, so why do you think *you* should? Adding new experiences or conversations with new people increases your knowledge pool, promoting increased brain activity. It stretches our resilience, because we naturally react to new stimuli, making us draw on our natural survival instinct, which becomes dormant if we remain unchallenged. Adaptability is like an anti-wrinkle cream for the brain.

YOU CAN LEARN FROM YOUR EARLY YEARS

I'm going to share with you a bit about my early years, to give you some context about my journey. The person you may have seen on television is only a small cog in a bigger wheel that drives me – where I've come from and how this has informed the person I've become, that inner child is still in there, deep down, providing the impetus I need to continue with my journey. Our lives as adults may look starkly different from the lives we had as children, but that doesn't mean any of it needs to be left behind. Instead, we can bring those experiences and lessons forward and let them shape the decisions we make about what we would like our lives to be like now, adapting our foundation so that it gives us something strong to stand on.

The first weeks of my life were spent living in a hostel with my mum. When she became pregnant out of wedlock, my grandmother wasn't happy, and my mum's stepfather, whom she didn't get on with at all, said she couldn't come back to the house. This left my mum giving birth to me alone, in hospital, on 27 August 1972. That in itself must have been hard, but to add to that, there were people circling around her, trying to get her to give me up for adoption while she was still lying in the hospital bed. Papers were being thrust in her face and she didn't understand what was happening. It wasn't until one kind nurse said, 'You need to find someone to say that you have a home, that you've got somewhere to go to, otherwise your baby will be taken into care.' At that point, she became very alert to what was happening and got herself together.

It wasn't until much later that I realised what this must have been like for my mum, as she didn't speak about it much. But then one day, only a few years ago, she was watching TV and there had been an investigation into the Irish mothers whose children had been taken into workhouses, and she told me that while watching it she broke down. She remembered how close she was to being one of those women whose babies were taken from them – signed away. And she told me how hard she'd had to fight. Some of the nurses were clearly disapproving and couldn't separate their judgements from the maternity care they were meant to be giving to her, apart from that one nurse who changed everything.

I believe there's always one person who will enter your life and give you that reset or renewed confidence, and it was that nurse at that moment for my mum. And, in many ways, for me: an early experience in the first days after I was born of someone having a positive impact on the trajectory of my life. It almost feels godly, as if someone had been sent to save us. I'm spiritual, rather than religious, but there's just a sense that she was a guardian angel, stepping in and saying one line that changed absolutely everything. My mum held me tight, got out of that hospital and found a hostel that we could stay in. My grandmother was sending her a little bit of money and some clothes for me, but the hostel was a very bleak place. Everyone there was struggling in some way, and soon other women were stealing from my mum. She felt scared and alarmed that other mothers would steal from her, so she knew she had to get out as soon as possible, which she did. She made a shift.

After a while, my godmother, who lived in Birmingham, took us in, and that was the first step of my mum rebuilding her life. She wanted more for herself and her new baby, and she understood that to achieve that she'd need to work for it. Those were the foundations she was raised on: an understanding that to create the life you'd like for yourself you must work hard. It was instilled from my great-grandmother in Jamaica, and reinforced by her three sisters, passed through to my grandmother who came to Britain in the 1950s, and who was a nurse for forty years. Thankfully, this passed to my mum, who immediately recognised that it would take all her strength of character to prove people wrong. She refused to be seen as a failure. She had come from a line of women who had to be self-reliant homemakers while raising their families, an all-too-familiar story in some parts of the Caribbean.

In some ways, when you look at my early years, you could say that the odds were stacked against us, as a unit, from the outset. Feeling inferior or with an embedded resentment could have bled into my identity. There was no male counterpart in the home, no father taking on those struggles or helping her. And my mum was trying to fit into a patriarchal society where women had to ask permission to get a mortgage, especially if you were unmarried.

She was doing all that and managing to run a home, raise a child, provide food, pay the bills and work full-time. I challenge anyone to think again if they assume that doesn't rub off on you in some way, or bury itself deep into your psyche as you are moving through life. Instead of focusing on the negative aspects of a situation, for my mum it was a choice not to sit in misery but to move forward. As the cliché goes: when the going gets tough – the tough get going!

The mental switch

How do you make a mental switch between negative and positive thinking when you have to adapt to a curveball or crisis?

- Negative thinking never solves anything. It's like a runaway train that can quickly build momentum. Be self-aware: once you catch your little negative demon, get a voice and start to create a dialogue with yourself; just say 'Stop it!' There is no magic, it's as simple as that. Identify and neutralise.
- Switch your focus to a thought or action that is step one to a positive move. It might mean calling

someone. Simply speaking to a person of trust, who will not catastrophise the situation, can help you to order your thought processes.

- Sometimes if you feel overwhelmed by the crisis, thinking about taking deep, long breaths will help to slow down your heart rate and add more oxygen into your body, thereby stopping your head from spinning.
- If you can walk or change your environment, do so. I have found this particularly helpful; a different stimulus can serve as the perfect distraction until you feel calmer.
- I have been known to listen to an empowering piece of music.
- Another tip is to give yourself a two-minute timer to create a window to breathe through all the negative energy. Once that time is over, move on to one of the above suggestions.

Reflecting on our childhood can be difficult, and some of you will find it tougher than others, but when we understand where we come from, we can learn to adapt not only to how the world sees us, but also to how we see ourselves — perhaps giving ourselves a little extra kindness, or an extra push. The layered early life experience with my mum taught me what it means to be resilient as a small child. In fact, when I was three, my nursery teacher, Wendy, remarked that she thought I would become the first female prime minister. Margaret Thatcher achieved this in the late 1970s, but I continue to be fascinated by nature versus nurture and whether it's a bit of both that promotes determination in an individual.

THE LESSONS I LEARNED OUTSIDE THE CLASSROOM

I became very mature for my age because of the responsibilities that I had to take on. My mum worked full-time and couldn't pick me up from school or be there when I got home, something that is largely frowned upon these days. She had tried to enlist help from a couple of parents to support me after school, but sadly that didn't work out: one parent had me cleaning while refusing to give me any food on a few too many occasions, so my mum called time on that. Instead, she had to trust me to look after my front-door key all day, come home, let myself in, make a sandwich, and do my homework – and that's exactly what I did.

Although I spent a lot of time on my own as a child,

I was very socialised, because from the age of six I went to dance classes twice a week and Sunday school at my local Methodist church, and when I was nine I became a member of my local athletics club. I never felt lonely and I liked my own company, too. I think I had an inner confidence. My daily routine gave me a format to get through each day when I wasn't doing activities. I didn't play outside much with other children, but rather I spent time learning about the world by reading my collection of *Encyclopaedia Britannica*, or practising my dance steps.

I remember my mum telling me about a distressing situation when she got caught unexpectedly in a heavy downfall of snow one winter on her way home. The buses were suspended and she couldn't get back from work, and I was at home awaiting her arrival. She was fretful as she walked for hours through the snow to make it home, unable to contact me because we didn't have a telephone landline, nor did she drive, and every sound of a police siren or ambulance made her heart rate soar. She recalls being tearful as she put the key in the door, unsure of what state I might be in, but she found me in my pyjamas sitting on our sofa just waiting patiently. I must have been a little concerned at one point, but my small routines that I was taught were ingrained and familiar, and they kept me preoccupied, calm and patient.

THE SKILL OF SELF-SOOTHING

Some would say that I was too independent, too soon, but I actually feel very grateful for those difficult early days; they made me grittier and more determined. I had to work out coping strategies for myself, build self-reliance and learn how to self-soothe, something I still do to this day. The ability to self-soothe allows you to distract yourself from feelings that could bring on concerns, worry or anxiety; it's a temporary solution that hopefully bridges a moment when you start to feel that you could become overwhelmed. Every day we will encounter situations that we will need to adapt to. Sometimes it might not be feasible to phone a friend. You might be in a board meeting, teaching at school, or with a supposed friend when an interaction didn't go well, or perhaps you are stuck in a car with a loved one having had a blazing row! What do you do? How do you cope and self-soothe in that instant?

- Change your environment. If you're outdoors, go somewhere familiar.
- If you're indoors, go and grab some fresh air; 20 minutes should do the trick.
- Breathe long and deep. If you're flustered, your heart rate will increase – try box breathing: inhale to the

count of four, hold for four seconds, exhale for four seconds, hold on to the out-breath for four seconds. This will help to lower your heart rate.

- When you can take a warm bath or shower, relax in the water – go with the flow of it. Natural elements have a profound way of restoring balance. Combined with some deep inhalations, this should be enough to calm you. You can always add essential oils for a deeper calming experience.

- Distract yourself with a dose of escapism, whether it's a good book or a comedy on a streaming channel, or listen to music that takes you back to a period in your life when you felt free and happy. Switching off your mind will offer you respite.

Although I became self-sufficient from a young age, I was always aware, possibly unconsciously, that I was important to my mum: I felt like her nucleus. My mum told me that it took ages to get me out of sharing her bed; I loved to nestle in and feel her warmth. We didn't have much money, and I remember that there was mould in the corner of my bedroom in the house we rented, which I calmly watched creeping up the wall, getting worse and worse, not realising that we couldn't afford to repair the issue. It was our home, and within it I felt very secure and loved. Perhaps the first building block of a secure, happy adult is to know that as a child you have one person who loves you, who is fighting your corner. My mum was that person for me. She never faltered in that.

MAKE A MOVE

After a few years in the rented, mouldy house, my mum managed to secure a mortgage and buy us a home. It was my mum's dream house on a new estate on the other side of town in Wolverhampton. She had always aspired to get away from the deprived area we lived in, but even more so from our dysfunctional neighbour. The new house was in an environment that felt much more family friendly. She was on her way to becoming a homeowner, which would form an important part of my mum's identity: it mattered to her to own her own house, a place where no one could tell her she didn't belong, giving her the stability that she'd craved since leaving the comfort and love of her grandmother in Jamaica, and she worked incredibly hard to achieve this. She was twenty-five years old.

Among the labels and history we are born with, we get to choose the identities we want to own – the one that sits right in our skin – but we must work towards it. Not just physically but mentally, too. My mum wanted to be a homeowner, and that meant taking on a second job, which meant I had less time with her, because she needed to keep things afloat now that the bills were higher, and scarier. With that risk came more stress, especially as it was all her responsibility as a single mother. I could see that she was determined to give me a better life. It was her sacrifice and commitment to providing her only child with the best she possibly could. She gave 100 per cent to everything. To others, what we had may have seemed very little, but I've always recognised and appreciated my mum's commitment. She was going without and giving up certain comforts in life in order to have something else. It's that constant trade-off – those balancing scales again – to find balance between roles, and the present and the future. This was something that I pondered as I navigated my teenage years with my athletics ambitions. How much was I willing to sacrifice? What could I afford to lose, to change, risk or adapt? Mum totally embodied the motto 'If you want something in life you have to work very hard to get it', and she's passed that down to me.

I don't remember yearning to have more time with my mum, although by the time I had reached my teens she had two jobs, a day and a night shift, and was home for only a matter of hours before she was off again. I accepted that it was something she had to do, and I turned all my focus to my athletics, which meant travelling to Birmingham a couple of nights a week. I became even more self-reliant, mobilising myself from school to training, then home again. I was on my own path, never bothering to look around me to wonder or feel envious of what other teenagers my age were doing. I just kept working hard, learning to be patient, my self-belief rising day by day. There was no second career in my head if being a sportswoman didn't work out – there was no Plan B.

As soon as I was able to get a job, I did, and I worked a monotonous nine-to-five job in a packing centre, waiting for the bell to ring so that I would get paid. Grateful to have some cash in my hand, I saved up for my driving lessons and eventually a car, to make my athletics life easier. I needed to pass my driving test first time, because I wouldn't have been able to afford a retest. Luckily, I did. Learning to be self-reliant, as I had had to do throughout my childhood, is a plus. Remember, that doesn't mean that you can't ask for help should you really need it, but working out problems on your own, or setting small tasks for yourself, is invigorating. I remember feeling a huge sense of pride collecting my second-hand car because I had taken the steps to make it happen.

You might start with small hurdles, but before you know it you'll be attacking the bigger hurdles with confidence. The self-reliance that was pushed upon me as a teen is a gift that keeps on giving, even at the age of fifty-one. When you look back at your teenage years, what character traits did you have then that are still present in your character today? Kindness, conscientiousness, good humour, honesty? Stop and have a think about the lessons from childhood that you've adapted into your current life and how they still help you today. When I talk about choosing what to bring forward and what to leave behind, this is the kind of thing I mean. Search for the positive elements from your past, even if they felt negative or unimportant at the time, and recognise how they have empowered you and given you certain skill sets that you might have taken for granted.

ALWAYS A WOMAN'S WOMAN

Having a powerful sense of sisterhood is an integral part of my identity: from my wonderful grandma, to my mum, to the close-knit GB athletes in my girl gang that shared the highs and lows of competitive life while miles away from home, and to the wonderful mums who have been here for me when I've panicked about missing a pick-up or getting to a playdate for one of my children. Female relationships have been important to me since my teens, when the absence of my mum because of her constant working meant that I looked for support in other people. My gratitude to those women who have helped craft my identity, giving me a feeling of safety and trust, means that one of the most important roles I play in this world is one that helps to motivate, elevate and comfort the sisterhood. Some of my closest friends have been by my side for more than thirty-five years, and women have shaped my thoughts, my ideals and my ideas more than any man has ever done. The role of friend is one that I take seriously. My good friends congratulate me on all the healthy adaptations I make in my life, as I celebrate theirs. They respect me and love me for who I am – all the different parts of who I am. We'll talk about this more later, but when a friend doesn't enjoy your success, query it. If a friend doesn't support the positive adaptations you are making in your life, take that on board. For some people, self-improvement in those around them can be a bitter pill to swallow: it holds up a mirror to all the changes they are *not* making in their own life. Never be that person. One of your duties as a friend is to applaud the adaptability of a friend who was stuck, or held back, and is now finding the courage to change her outlook and outcomes.

Superwoman

Leanne Pero

I met Leanne in the autumn of 2020 when I was asked to present her an award for her charitable work in the community on health and well-being. She told me all about the charity she had founded, Black Women Rising, whose aim is to encourage women from Black and Asian communities to be more breast-cancer aware by promoting the importance of breast checks to help with early detection of the disease, signposting to support services, and offering a space for people to share their cancer journeys.

I was immediately struck by her story and how she turned the challenging experience of being diagnosed with breast cancer in her early thirties into a lifeline for other women. Her drive and determination kept her going when many around her didn't understand why setting up a charity to educate women from ethnically diverse communities was even necessary. Now in its fifth year, the charity is going from strength to strength, thanks to Leanne's strong sense of sisterhood and resilience, and her drive to help others. I asked her to share her story.

DENISE What do you think makes one person sit back and accept a situation but another to act? What motivated you to start your own charity?

LEANNE I was quite oblivious to the way that healthcare professionals were when I was diagnosed with breast cancer. My background is mixed race, my mum is mixed race and she was adopted by two white people. I grew up in Norfolk for a lot of my life, and I knew about racism across the board but not really about racism when it comes to medical care. When my mum first had breast cancer, I was young, but when I was diagnosed, my mum had been diagnosed for a second time six months before me. My journey was a little bit easier than my mum's first experience of cancer because everyone in the hospital knew her and we were together the majority of the time. But when I was going through it, and she was sitting with me on the chemo ward, we started to see how women who were Black African or Caribbean, and had strong accents, were being misunderstood. Part of our culture is to ask questions and be quite loud, which some healthcare professionals dismissed as being rude or difficult, which it wasn't – for many of these women, it was the first time that they'd heard the word 'cancer'. They were scared. The next thing Mum and I noticed on the chemo ward was that there were so many black ladies there by themselves. At the time, we were allowed to bring a few people with us, but these women were on their own, because their family didn't know that they could come in and support them. I realised there was a huge discrepancy of care, but the biggest issue wasn't the care itself. Obviously, we were so grateful we were receiving it; if we had gone anywhere else in the world it would have cost us over £200,000. But it was the lack of cultural understanding that was a problem for us. When I saw this inequity going on in the cancer world, I was motivated to set up a movement for these women. My immediate thoughts are always to give back, make positive changes and build positive places, because I didn't have them while growing up. I didn't have a safe space then, and I didn't have a safe space while I was going through cancer. I had great family and friends, but it was a very isolating and lonely place, particularly as a black woman. Trauma is a massive driver for people. You can sink or swim with trauma. I refused to sink, so I had to fight it.

DENISE When I think back to my mum's generation, my grandma's generation, they had to be resilient and overcome trauma, or they would go down. If they didn't fight, there was no one there to save them.

LEANNE My sister is thirty-five. She's been through a lot of traumas, and we were exposed to our parents' trauma. We were discussing the idea of *where does it stop?* Why are we, as women of colour, consistently in this fight-or-flight mode of having to fight, having to overcome trauma, having to heal? I've got to a point where I'm sick and tired of things being hard. When is it going to get easier? Luckily, I have resilience, because if you don't, where do you go? Who's going to have your back?

DENISE Childhood traumas can get compounded by experiences in adulthood. Take the workplace, where women of colour are having to deal with not being seen for their abilities, getting overlooked for promotions, then having to self-soothe to get through the hostilities they face. How do we learn to adapt to this environment in order to survive?

LEANNE It takes a lot of self-care and a lot of therapy. Three years ago, I had a three-month mental breakdown. Because of my work with Black Women Rising, I was seeing death on a daily basis, and I knew that it was getting to me, but I didn't expect to experience a complete crash. I remember a couple of things I was told by various people around that time. Firstly, if you're not going to look after yourself, you can't do this work any longer. I had to put some serious things in place. I was in therapy, but I realised that wasn't enough to do the work I was doing, so I adapted my well-being care to get a proper trauma-informed therapist – someone who deals with death and trauma from sexual abuse victims. Secondly, I looked at my holistic care: what am I eating, what am I putting into my body on a daily basis? I began weekly acupuncture and found some amazing fitness people. But self-care takes money, you know? I didn't have the resources, but I thought: *In order for me to do the work that I do, I've got to put certain things in place.*

Leanne's resilience toolkit

- I wouldn't be here without my therapist, without my fitness plan, without my nutrition knowledge or without my acupuncturist. You are worth the self-investment.
- I cleared away a lot of negative, toxic people around me. People from way back in the day, some of those friends who sat with me in the chemo ward but later became jealous of my success.
- I was in a romantic relationship that had to go.
- I started doing mini-gratitude practices, during which I thought about my wants and needs, and what made me happy. What is serving me and what is not?

- I prayed. I have a prayer partner with whom I pray every morning. It's quite regimented and strict.
- I believe that there is power in being regimented with routines.

Putting those things in place allowed me to show up authentically. I want to show up for my loved ones and my charity, I want to feel great, I want to live in the moment – and I want to feel. Before cancer, I remember saying to a mentor who I had at the time, 'I'm achieving a lot for my age, but I don't feel it, I don't feel great.' It was because I had so much trauma, so much build-up, so now everything for me is about joy, and the minute it's not joyful I just get rid of it.

DENISE Growth is about finding your own best practice and your own routines. For all of us, it's about understanding ourselves more and knowing what's going to strengthen us.

LEANNE We can all become the master of ourselves. We get to choose our own identities. We have to stop letting others impose their views on us without knowing our background stories. And we have to give ourselves the gift of living in the moment and looking to the future. I've got to a point where I no longer really speak about cancer. Do we need to keep going over what has happened? Do we need to keep going over the traumas in life? Or do we keep going forward? Because I don't keep talking about trauma, I've been told a few times, mainly from black and brown people, that I might be unrelatable to others. I get that; they're seeing my life now: I'm enjoying myself, I'm living for joy, I'm putting myself in spaces and places, I'm doing things, and partly I'm doing it because I'm not focusing on the trauma. I won't use my past as a way to get likes or validations, or more speaking gigs, or all these other things that are out there as trauma porn.

DENISE We are more than what has happened to us in the past, but it is a choice, and it's our choice. It's ironic that we try to be a beacon of light for our black and brown sisters, but there are points at which we are told we are sell-outs because we want to move, flap our wings or extend our circles.

LEANNE It's something that plagues all of us as we're moving up that ladder. It's so sad that we have to deal with this from our own community as successful black women. A word I have been leaning on recently is 'integrity'. In everything that I do, I am governed by that one word, because I know my source and I know why I do the work that I do. It's very tempting to step outside that box and do what other people are doing. But I'm focused on the integrity of my identity.

DENISE When I'm being bombarded by people telling me what I should be doing, my gut instinct has been my main driver – coming back to how something or someone makes me feel. What do I want to do? What do I trust? Is this really aligning with my values? Then I make my decision. How have you learned to trust your gut and back yourself?

LEANNE I put in that self-care. I've allowed myself to focus on self-care. All those little things that I spoke about (the exercising, the therapy) have allowed my mind some breathing space to be in my thoughts, to soak into who I am. Ask yourself, 'How am I feeling today?' Have that mental check-in. Exercise those little muscles around your gut instinct to help you feel the difference between fight-or-flight mode, and recognise when you're not feeling great. The more you get to know yourself, the more you will get comfortable with yourself, and the stronger your gut instinct will become. Even if you can just give yourself one hour a day, in the morning before the kids get up perhaps, to start doing spiritual practices, that will help. Yes, it takes discipline, and yes, you'll be tired, but that's one hour a day for yourself. I'm forty next year, and the number of people my age, my peers, who don't know who they *really* are is shocking. They never do things for themselves – everything is about everybody else. And what people haven't yet started to grasp is the importance of being selflessly selfish. It's so important as a mother, as a wife, as a friend, to put yourself and your needs at the forefront a lot of the time. That means carving out *you* time. When women come to me and ask for business advice, I always ask them, 'What time you are investing in yourself?' And for those struggling, I would say to start off small, with that one ungodly hour from 5 until 6am, getting up and starting a positive routine.

DENISE Age is a great thing, because we become more comfortable standing in our own power and caring less about what other people think of us. The sooner we get that self-awareness, the sooner we can make better decisions for ourselves going forward. How can we get there quicker?

LEANNE It starts today. Small wins. Start small. If you've got a list of things you want to change and it gets overwhelming, start with one thing. Measure it; for example, I managed to lose 7 pounds (3.17kg) just before my holiday. I probably put it all back on on my holiday, but I lost it. I made a checklist, and every day that I didn't eat crisps I gave myself a tick, and that gave me such satisfaction! Look, I've got seven ticks in a row, and that was something for me to celebrate.

DENISE We need to celebrate small achievements – they propel us towards bigger ones.

LEANNE I noticed, doing my work in dance, how young people, especially those from poor backgrounds, didn't know what the feeling of achievement felt like. In my dance classes I set up small wins for them, such as by the end of term they performed in front of parents. Everyone has to do that at the end of those ten weeks, and we praise and celebrate them, we allow them to have that feeling of achievement. In every lesson plan there is a box where we ask the teacher, 'How are you going to motivate and praise the kids?' A lot of my research was around how many young people just didn't have a sense of feeling good about themselves and that sense of achievement. Motivation and praise are so important, but as an adult you get them less from external sources – and you have to do it to yourself. Self-praise, self-achievement – these have to be at number one, otherwise you go out there and look for other people to do it for you, and it won't happen. It isn't even going to come from a partner – that's additional! It's got to come from yourself.

————

YOU ARE WHAT YOU DO

There might be a moment in our lives, or careers, when we think: *OK, I'm on the right path. This is going to be where I'm staying for a while at least.* Or when we realise that we're not on the right path and that now is the time to change it. For some people this requires a little more confidence, or to believe that the opportunity will arise. For others, they can step out with ease, striding forward and making changes without a second thought. But who do you really want to be? Who are you deep down, or when you take your make-up off and get into bed every night? In this world of social media, it's easy to invent an identity for likes or attention, but is that healthy? In the short term, yes, you might get a little endorphin lift from the visible adoration, but knowing your true self – your values, your goals and what makes you happy – is more important than the quick boost you get from being adored by people you'll never meet. During a period of serious adaptation, don't look or listen too much to the whirling opinions around you, look inwards. Yes, a big career change, or moving to another city or country, or getting divorced, is scary, but there is also freedom in getting to choose a new identity for yourself. How do you want to adapt to what life has thrown at you?

I was forced to reinvent myself when I retired from professional sports. Depending on your sport, you can enter your first retirement phase by your mid- to late twenties, for others it can be early to mid-thirties. It can be a daunting time, as it would be for anybody moving into uncharted territory at any age, but I do think that the challenge for athletes is heightened because so much of their identity is wrapped up in behaviour, lifestyle, routines and discipline. This could be one of the reasons why some athletes compete for too long. I know that I went through months of soul-searching wondering whether I would find true contentment again and an identity that would bring me satisfaction.

Initially, it was just a sweet relief to not have to train so hard all the time, but that swiftly turned into, 'Oh my God, what do I do next?' I didn't have anything lined up, and I spent three years in what I call The Wilderness. I remember calling Baroness Sue Campbell, a trailblazer in sport, who I got to know in her role as chair of the Youth Sports Trust, a brilliant charity that educates and empowers young people through play. I went into her office for a long chat, and she invited me to do some work with the Trust, which gave me the sense of purpose I needed during that time of change. Going to people who know what is important to you, such as educating kids on the importance of fitness, can really help you to adapt in order to reassess your goals and rebuild confidence.

From that point on, I did a brief and terrifying stint as a TV sports reporter in the Midlands. I wasn't ready for the speed at which they expected me to learn to present live on TV, and they threw me in the job at the deep end, which gave me a sink-or-swim feeling. I'm not a perfectionist, but I like to do a good job – and I know that I did not. I was really awful. But, amazingly, I got a phone call from BBC Sports who said that they'd love me to join their team as an athletics commentator. That felt like a better fit for me. After all, I had been commentated on all through my career, so I said yes, perhaps naively. It was only when I was on set that I realised how much harder it is than it looks: you have to talk to guests in the studio, while being spoken to through your earpiece, and stay looking engaged, making sense and thinking ahead to your next question. I remember answering a question live on air from my then editor that should have been posed to a studio guest. In the early days my brain felt quite scrambled. I had to learn a lot about compartmentalising and concentration, but I adapted and got the hang of it.

Over the last fifteen years, the job hasn't changed, but I

have. I've become more confident, a bit more self-assured about who I am and what I bring to the coverage I'm presenting, whereas in the beginning, I was very mindful that I was working for the BBC! 'I don't sound very BBC', 'Do I sound right?', 'Do I look right?', 'How do I fit in?' The person that guided me at the start was Colin Jackson: he showed me the ropes and made sure that I was where I needed to be, but – as always – you have to figure out the job yourself. There are no shortcuts. You might receive a bit of steering, a bit of scaffolding, but you have to face the climb yourself – in any employment position.

When you're facing the end of a career that has formed a huge part, if not all, of your identity, it's important to work out what else can make you spark, and be open-minded enough to try something new. Feeling purposeful is a strong driver for many, and I remember that although I had married my partner, Steve, and we were growing our family and it was all very exciting and new, I still felt that being an ex-athlete defined me, even when I joined the BBC team in 2009. I was surrounded by a host of ex-athletes, and yet I still felt naked, exposed and vulnerable, because I didn't feel that I had fully owned my space and new identity (I talk more about this in Chapter 5).

The ability to step out of your comfort zone and change direction is a demonstration of adaptability. Once you get past the initial confusion and fear, you will be able to unleash a side of your character that you didn't know about, or a skill that you hadn't had a chance to explore before. A change in career is possibly one of the best identity boosts that you can gift yourself: a professional challenge and change reminds you that you are alive and constantly evolving.

AN IDENTITY BOOST

The day that Seb Coe called me up to be part of the presentation team that was to travel to Singapore for the London 2012 Olympics bid is a day that I will never forget, and came at a crucial time for me. I was still functioning on a low ebb, having retired from competing, and although flattered by his request, I was riddled with imposter syndrome. It was more than a fear of failing, it was dealing with an identity shift that I was uncomfortable with, coupled with the thought that that role could only belong to a certain type of individual with a university degree who had the skill set to deliver a stirring speech. Nevertheless, I knew that I couldn't turn down such a wonderful opportunity.

The problem wasn't really my ability, it was more about conquering a fear that I had as a child: reading aloud. I used to dread that moment in English lessons when it was time to read a chapter from the class novel. My teacher would make us stand and read from the current chapter. Awful. But there I was, fresh off the plane and in Singapore, this girl from Wolverhampton presenting to the International Olympic Committee and representing Queen and country. I remember standing there with the rest of the British contingent: the late, great Tessa Jowell, Ken Livingstone (the mayor of London at the time), Lord Coe, one of my childhood heroes, and Sir Keith Mills (a successful entrepreneur and multimillionaire). Sir Keith had revealed to me that he left school with no qualifications, and this confirmed to me that you cannot let your past hold you back – you get to choose who you want to be.

I conquered my fear, and I didn't falter in the presentation. Neither did any of the team members, and the rest, as they say, is history. We won the bid, and London 2012 was a roaring success! That day, I stood there, knowing I could do it, despite *just* being that girl from Wolverhampton. From that moment on, I knew that I could stand up and be myself in any room, in front of anyone. I had earned it. I promised myself that I would not shy away from putting myself forward for speaking engagements in the future. Although it would still take me a few more years to feel fully at home with public speaking and giving presentations in the corporate arena, I do cite that very first time in Singapore, when so much was riding on it, as an identity boost. It was a moment to step into the unknown – recognising that there was fear, but the results from it allowed me to find a voice where I could share my thoughts and experiences on topics that are important to me.

 take an identity health check

Make a note of your answers to the following:

1. Am I on the right path?
2. Do I need to change anything right now?
3. Am I content with where I am?
4. What can I improve?

My ambassadorial work for various charities, combined with becoming a board member for events such as the London 2017 Athletics Championships and the Commonwealth Games England (for which I served as president for eight years), has broadened my impact and reach to a wider group of people. It has also added another strand to my profile while elevating my understanding of governance within sport, which will benefit my current term as President of UK Athletics. I'll be in the role for a few years, and it is truly one of the greatest honours of my life, to be serving the sport that has given me so much, and it provides a new identity to add to the others in my life, and one that I could never have imagined I would have achieved as a young girl.

Five things that could boost your identity today

1. See adaptability as your superpower. Challenge yourself to make changes that you know will give you a boost, not just externally but internally, too.

2. Find ways in which you can extend what you believe is possible in your work environment and in your spare time. It might be finding a new activity, putting your name down to volunteer for something, or applying for a position at work that you might think is beyond your reach but you know that you could learn to do a great job.

3. Experiment, have fun, and try things out for size. It could be something small like a new hairstyle. For those that may have followed my career, changing my hairstyles is seasonal, it's ever-changing, and

I love the lift that it gives me to feel renewed – a fresh start that sometimes necessitates a wardrobe change to complement my new style or colour. I know it's my thing and not for everyone, but they do say, 'look good, feel good', and I know that this is a simple way to feel differently about yourself, even if it's superficial.

4. Look for a new mentor or a new community that lifts and empowers you, and whose values and goals are similar to yours.

5. Sit still for a moment and note down where you see yourself in a month, in a year, in a decade. Thinking and planning ahead will pull everything into focus, but we – especially women – are so bad about giving ourselves the time to do that. Leanne Pero talks a lot about putting good energy out into the world to receive it, and I hear many athletes talking about manifesting their dreams. If you say positive things to yourself, you feel good; if you feel good, you will act more positively; if you act more positively, you will be open to receiving good energy by controlling your outlook on life and becoming who you were meant to be.

No big career change comes without curveballs getting thrown your way. Just as you're celebrating a success, you might discover that something else has pushed you two steps back. This is rubbish, but it's the reality. We can't control everything, but we can adapt to the unexpected. When I've been faced with an identity crisis or professional setback of some sort, I've learned the following: I face the challenge head-on (what needs to be done? Who do I need to talk to? How much am I able to do right now?); I get clear on the steps involved in dealing with the unexpected situation (this might be a few hours, or days or weeks, or even longer); and I remember that careers – and life – are a roller coaster and we have to ride the lows as well as the highs.

HOW MOTHERHOOD CAN AFFECT YOUR IDENTITY

As we've discussed above, identity is informed by our up-bringing, our friends, the career we choose, the choices we make and how we adapt as we move through life. When something new comes along – motherhood, for example – we shift and evolve in ways we might not recognise initially because the role of motherhood is expected to be a natural process, one you decided upon. There's an unspoken agreement that a woman is meant to give up everything she is to this new blessing, and not only to make room for this new part of her identity, but also to make it the most important one.

I worked hard to become an athlete, battled injuries and worked my ass off to get to the top, but being a mum is the hardest role I've ever taken on. Motherhood is a *whole* different type of hard work, and one that I'm still learning a lot about. The role of mother has taken me on so many roller coasters that no book, documentary or course could prepare me for. It has taught me about willpower, self-sacrifice and adaptability like nothing else ever has. It has challenged my values and expectations, at times consuming me both physically and mentally.

The biggest trick I've learned in balancing my identity as a mother with the other roles I play is to compart-mentalise effectively; giving myself a chance to strike a balance between my children's needs and my own. You've heard of the term 'mummy guilt'? It's real. Quieting that internal voice (mothers tend to be their own harshest critic) *and* the external voices that want to judge you, take a lot of grit to fight against. I've had to learn to give myself permission to take time out, to take myself off-duty, and to know that everyone will actually be OK. They'll survive, perhaps even thrive with a bit of time away from my over-caring. It took me a little while to get to this point, my role model being my mum, who was so self-sacrificing that she didn't find balance until very late in her life, motherhood forming the biggest part of her identity into her retirement years, despite me leaving home at twenty-four.

I have four children, ranging in age from early twenties down to six years old. Motherhood is definitely a huge part of my identity, and I am always interested in looking at how different women adapt in that role, and in their family. The longer we are in it, I think the more it tends to reshape us. I went from being a career woman, and central in my own life, to being a mother who spent a large portion of her time – the majority of her time – focused on putting her children's needs first, mind, body and soul. How could I juggle these two very important identities? Honestly, at times I've felt overwhelmed, trying to find a balance, but the sooner you can recognise that you can't get parenting 100 per cent right all the time (you can work to a better ratio of 80:20 and cut yourself some slack), the easier the juggle will be. This has been a hard lesson for me to grasp when most of my athletics career has been striving for perfect execution. At times, being able to deliver my best for my kids has been unrealistic – largely because we are not only dealing with our own personality but also the personalities of our little people – plus our partner.

HOLDING ON TO *YOU*

Working out how much of yourself you're willing to sacrifice, and for how long, is a big dilemma for most women who recognise that they need more than life inside the home and family unit. How much are you willing to compromise? The more children you have, the bigger the compromise, and the more you have to stretch and adapt. Finding time for yourself can feel impossible at times, especially when they're young, or when they're teens and you're pushed into the role of taxi driver.

Don't get me wrong, I made the choice to have four children, and it's been beautiful watching these little humans develop and grow into lovely young adults, like Lauryn, Kane and Ryan have, with little Troy shooting up at the rear. But I recognise how much mental energy I have given away, and there is a point when we have to call time and tend to ourselves in order to survive parenting in this digital age, when increasing demands on parents to safeguard and scaffold young lives from home have become more crucial. Gone are the days when teachers were there to teach, and parents could somewhat disconnect to focus on providing love and sustenance. Having two neurodivergent children means learning the best practices to support them at school, adding an extra complexity to the support they need at home. My patience levels have had to adapt massively. Like so many women, I am the diary maker, travel coordinator and health and well-being officer within the home: signposting, negotiating, and taking the brunt of the resistance from rightfully stroppy teenagers.

It doesn't take long for the stress to mount up in a very active household. There comes a point when you have to surrender and raise the white flag, and take action to save yourself. School runs, extra-curricular activities, running a home, working and domestic conflict started to take its toll on my mood. When you've come from a childhood where you've seen struggle, you can stay in that struggle mode for too long, because in a funny way you're used to it. Women need to get better at nurturing themselves.

Mums need to remember . . .

- You are not a robot, so don't be ashamed to seek help and ask for the tools you need to cope.
- Admitting to yourself that things are tough before they become chronic is a must.
- If you are snappy and disgruntled, that's usually a sign that you are unhappy. What can you adapt?
- Identify the route of your happiness.
- Share the load and give up some control.

- Explain your values and why certain values are important to your partner, if you have one, and your children.
- Discuss a better job-share around the home – despite what they might tell you, others in the house can see when the dishwasher needs emptying or the laundry needs to be put away. Refuse to allow your other important identities (career woman, friend, runner, reader, whatever other roles are important to you) to get swallowed up by housework and other people's expectations about what you have to be now. Find your own flow.

In terms of my identity as a mother, particularly the first time round, there were challenges that I had to overcome internally and externally because I didn't have the emotional or logistical support from my athletics federation. I remember asking for permission to take my then two-year-old daughter to the preparation camp for the 2004 Olympic Games, and it was made very clear to me that she wouldn't be welcome. Yes, I could find neighbouring accommodation and stay in a different place with Lauryn from the rest of Team GB, and I would be allowed to have lunch with the rest of the Olympians, and obviously use the training facilities, but that was it. I didn't question this; instead I was grateful that I was granted authorisation to be there, not yet fully able to own my dual identities as an athlete *and* mother.

The language of facilitating athlete mothers was not forthcoming then, in contrast to how it is today. There has been much improvement – there were crèche facilities at the 2024 Olympic Games in Paris, for example – and more sportswomen are taking more informed routes to dovetailing their careers with motherhood. I see this across most professions and industries, thank goodness. Now, if you're returning to work after having a baby, there is usually more in place to support you in terms of maternity pay and being able to request flexible working. That said, women still face discrimination in various guises. I imagine that it's particularly prevalent among first-time mums, because that's when we're at our most vulnerable and when people might take advantage of us. We're coming to terms with having been through pregnancy and birth, sleep deprivation and our bodies changing – and our confidence might have been affected, noticing that people are treating us differently. If then, to add to that, our workplace is unsupportive, it can really knock us down.

It's so important that you have a couple of supportive people to help you in the early days and weeks of being a working mum, particularly if you need a sounding board. Talking is a lifeline. Know your rights, as a mother, in terms of maternity leave, maternity pay and timelines for returning to work. Accept all the help and support you can get. And do some work around your new identity as a working mother. Being a parent doesn't need to become *everything* that you are, if that's not what you want. Yes, it is very much a part of you and your life now, and this can be something you embrace and feel proud of, but you can also have career goals and professional aspirations – even if you have to adapt to this new life by slowing down for a few years, or coming to a stop until the kids go to school. Being an adaptable mum with ambitions outside the home has certainly become a big part of who I am: I've taken back the reins with my career and shifted in a different direction, while still being ambitious, but not at the expense of supporting my children.

Own your motherhood path

- What do you want your path to look like? Your happiness matters too, so think about what next steps would make *you* feel fulfilled, not just those around you.
- Are your decisions financially driven or through pressure from your partner? Work out your budgets, what you spend and what you need.

- Make sure that your plan if you want to return to work is realistic – now probably isn't the time to take on a role that means being in a different city every day.
- Be flexible. It's OK to take a breather from the workspace if you can afford it, and you want to. It doesn't mean that you have failed. And it is OK to change your mind after going back to work if you realise you want to be at home with your child for a while.
- Don't allow yourself to be devalued if you choose to step away from your career for a while. Being a stay-at-home parent is rewarding if that aligns with your core values. Staying at home could be an avenue to starting something new. Other stay-at-home parents might have some great ideas to make the experience easier, so don't be afraid to reach out.
- There is much better support for working mothers now. Get clear on your employment rights as a parent, what government help is available, and ask working mothers you admire for their parenting hacks.

It was definitely easier when I became a mother for the second and third time. I knew what to expect, and having relatively easy pregnancies also made a difference. Steve and I moved house, my broadcasting career was on the increase in preparation for London 2012, and my family life was full on, but when you're in your mid-thirties you have the bandwidth and energy to cope. By the time I had my fourth child, Troy, I was in my late forties. I had to think of myself, my energy and my capacity, much more: just how was I going to balance everything when I was a so-called 'geriatric mum'? One positive benefit to being older was my mental approach: I had more confidence and a firmer understanding of what was needed to reimagine our home life and my career. During those early years with Troy, after spending twenty years building up my brand, I was a bit more clinical about setting out what I could and would achieve professionally, alongside becoming a mother all over again.

I wonder if there is more pressure for women to get back to work in this era? Is there more pressure for women in the public eye to get back to work as soon as they have their babies? If you're self-employed, there are still few provisions set up to offer financial security. A self-employed mum will not be earning any money if she chooses to take time away from work, whereas employed women who choose to have children will benefit from maternity benefits and a job to return to, with a monthly salary, after the maternity period. Neither choice is easy, however. Whatever path you choose, or can afford to take as a mum, you have to ask yourself some important questions.

 Your identity in motherhood

Make a note of your answers to the following:

1. Was it hard to take on the new identity of 'mother' or 'mum' while still trying to hold on to your career? Did it change how you viewed your work?
2. How did it impact your career? Think about the positives and negatives.
3. Did you embrace the tidal shift to your life, or did you find it overwhelming?
4. How well supported were you in early motherhood, in the home and at work?
5. What have you learned about yourself since becoming a mother?

VALUE YOURSELF

There's one last thing that I would like to cover in this chapter about maintaining identity, and that is your values: the things in life that matter most to you. Perhaps it's family or your work ethic, or perhaps you consider teamwork, kindness, compassion, agility or strength to be one of your key values. Perhaps you value integrity, creativity or calmness. Your values should be what govern your decision making and inform how you conduct yourself. Your values are your North Star: always guiding you to the light and guiding you home. How can you work out what yours are?

- Firstly, you need to think hard and deeply about what really matters to you, in life.
- Next, it's about looking at the ways you honour these values, in your day-to-day life; for example, if family is a value you cherish, are you spending enough time with yours? Are you creating the memories you hope that they will remember and cherish, which may eventually become the bedrock of their values? If luxury is up there, are you actually enjoying the luxuries you afford yourself? I hear from my friends with big houses that they often use only a few rooms in their mansions on a daily

basis, and once their children have flown the nest, they are rattling around in a big house that feels quite empty, often wondering why they've spent so much money on acquiring and furnishing their home. Perhaps this is nothing to do with values but status and ego.

- Being able to distinguish between what is ego and what is a set of true core values really helps to shape your behaviour, preventing you from potentially being drawn into areas that don't enhance you or your purpose and might lead you to act and interact with others differently.

- Make a distinction between what is part of your guiding principles as opposed to material needs and wants. What challenges or tests your value system? How does this affect your identity? You've got to find that inner peace.

I value integrity, kindness, independence, acceptance of difference, and loyalty. And I make sure that I'm honouring these areas as I move through life, in all my different roles. I don't place much emphasis on material items and never have. I like what I like, and I have my own sense of style, which I can maintain affordably, but I don't necessarily feel as if I have to wear labels. That's really not my bag. I do drive a nice car, though, because driving is my sanctuary.

It's when I listen to my music the most, or a podcast, and I connect with myself.

The fact that I feel pretty good about who I am and how I communicate with those around me is testament to how much I live by my values; even when holding them dearly creates conflict with others who don't see the world in the same way as me, I can be confident in my choices.

Now, in my fifties, I feel really strongly placed in my womanhood, more than at any other time in my life. There's a nice balance between my past achievements in athletics and how I've transitioned away from competitive sport. I've found new projects that test and stimulate me, which I believe keeps me fresh. Mentoring and helping others in areas that I feel passionate about is food for my soul. Despite a handful of mistakes I might have made in my past, I now have better clarity about who I am and what I need.

All women are beautiful complex creatures, and I hope we all find more self-acceptance with time, more self-confidence. When we stand strong in our identities, we can unveil our complete selves – the greatest blessing that comes from ageing. By finding the right steps early enough, through the lessons I share with you in this book, my hope is that you will learn to ask the right questions of yourself (and those around you) earlier than I did. I hope that by sharing my story you will be able to steer your own journeys more effectively, minimising fear or uncertainty, and feel closer to the person you were always meant to be.

 think about your values and identity

Make a note of your answers to the following:

1. What are your values?
2. How do you honour them?
3. Are your values part of your identity?
4. How would you like to present yourself to the world?
5. What new values would you like to focus on in the next stages of your journey?

In my moments of doubt, I look at where I've come from, the progress I've made, the successes I've had, the failures I've overcome and the people I've helped, and this pacifies me. I deserve to be exactly where I am in life because I've worked hard for it. And if something's not working out for me any more, I feel I have the confidence to change it. Yes, your identities and values form the core of who you are – mind, body and soul – but they are always evolving, always adaptable.

EMBRACE YOUR UNIQUENESS

Being a woman of colour and an only child raised by a single mum, I grew up aware that I was a little different from most of the people around me, and I suppose it comes as no surprise, post-athletic career, that I still stand out and represent a minority group in many of the circles I find myself in. I have conflicting feelings about this. I want to embrace my past, and the life experiences and heritage that makes me *me*, but I also want to feel that I belong and fit in without having to make so much effort. These confusing emotions around my identity have always been there. I remember being the sportiest girl at secondary school and going up to receive awards and recognition, and part of me was proud, but the other part of me didn't want to stand out – and sometimes I still don't want to stand out.

It's important that I do, however, and not just for those who look to me for inspiration or direction but for myself, too. I've grown to embrace the uniqueness of who I am, and I urge you to embrace *your* uniqueness, too. Instead of concentrating on the negative aspects – who you are not, what you don't have, what you lack or how you are different – allow yourself to think about the progress you have made, and the individuality you bring to the table. I don't think we are always fully aware of the impact we have on

71

others. We all have the capacity to be influencers, change makers and champions of positivity!

In Chapter 5, I explain more about how there is only one you and how important it is to understand who you are and to recognise your own personal boundaries. Sometimes, it's important to retreat, resist succumbing to FOMO and just be unashamedly you, while also adapting to different environments. I explain how it comes back to looking at your values and what's actually important in your life; for example, I have been told so many times that I need to post on social media much more than I do to be 'of influence' and to hit that magical 100k followers. That would, apparently, lead to more opportunities for partnering with big brands. But this comes at a price, and one my values won't allow me to pay. Spending even more time on the phone, when I complain about the amount of time my kids are on theirs, would make me a hypocrite, and I would lose some integrity! Boosting my audience and producing more content would be pretty time-consuming, and after looking at the time I had available on a weekly basis – between the school run, my presenting work, being a board member, extra-curricular pick-ups and drop-offs, school homework and chores – I decided this was much lower on my priorities list than others might think it should be, and right now I'm OK with that. I'm not saying this won't change and that I'll have to adapt to the growing demand for a strong social-media presence, but right here and now, recognising that I have a busy existence keeps me grounded in my expectations. When you feel pushed and pulled in ways that you're not sure about, I recommend writing a list of your non-negotiables – your values – and deciding what will fit and what won't. Then stick to your guns. You're the boss.

A big part of my identity that has had to be malleable since my retirement from athletics is my relationship with fitness and how important it is to me. For thirty-five years, it was what I did, and when I retired from athletics in 2005, I played tennis and golf occasionally, and joined fitness classes at my local gym from time to time but without any real consistency and motivation. I found it hard to see the benefit when I didn't have an end goal and a mission statement attached to it. I used the demands of family life as an excuse to opt out, and I watched from the sidelines as my husband indulged his time whenever and how often he liked in the recreational sports of his choice. Looking back, that was a *me* problem. Don't get me wrong, I was heavily occupied with raising a family, but I gave too much away physically, which I'm sure impacted my tolerance and mental stability at the time.

I was doing what I thought the wife and mother role ought to be, which is to be self-sacrificing – believing that the more you give, the more you will be valued and respected, and most of all appreciated. It doesn't really work like that, though, does it? I slowly found that out to my detriment, but it would take a few years until I had an awakening that the role of family martyr wasn't working for me, and I was allowed to reclaim some time and space for myself – which I'll be discussing further in Chapter 5. Women need to remember that in order to function well and rebalance all the energy you give out to others in daily life, you need to rebuild your own reserves.

These days, I do online classes from my small gym in the garden, saving travel time and money in the process. My family knows which are my exercise days and when I need their support in order to stick with them. They don't necessarily volunteer themselves, and being teenagers, they don't usually surface until after midday on weekends, but I've improved my asking skills. When volunteers are not forthcoming, you've got to ask for help and not assume that everyone knows what you need – and what you need is to understand what is best for you and how to advocate for yourself. Think about what self-care you need in place to feel good. What gives you energy? What gives you the dopamine boost that you desire? Write a list at the back of the book and incorporate those things as many times as is realistic to your lifestyle.

Five ways to adapt your identity for what you need today

1. Remember that you get to choose which parts of your childhood you bring forward and what you get to leave behind.

2. Honour the inner child and your roots but be whoever you want to be as an adult. You are not a mirror image of your parents, you are not trapped in a culture, or stuck in a social class.

3. If part of your identity feels missing (home life, work life), work out what it is and bring it in. Don't sacrifice yourself in order for others to live their lives. Nurture yourself, too.

4. Know that just because you've been holding one identity for a long time, it doesn't mean that you can't change and evolve. Humans wouldn't have survived if we weren't, at our core, flexible and versatile beings.

5. It's never too late to try something – or to be someone – new. The past doesn't have to hold you back. Just ask my golfing, sociable, explorative mum.

CHAPTER 2

Build Resilience

Do not judge me by my success, judge me by
how many times I fell down and got back up
again.

NELSON MANDELA

No dreams or goals ever materialise with a click of the fin-
gers. Winning takes work. Hard work – and it often takes
a very long time. Before embarking on any adaptation to
your life, you need to factor in the difficulty and the duration – and whether or not you have the endurance to keep
at it. There will be adversity, disappointment, stress, and
even some traumas along the way, but how you recover and
navigate through those difficult situations is an indicator

of how resilient you are. That's the tough talk done – now I want you to know that when you build your resilience and get a grip on your grit, you can take on the world, and in this chapter, I'm going to teach you some of the ways I found to do just that.

Let me share a story about one of my closest friends, Denise. We grew up together in Wolverhampton, and were inseparable at school – the two Denises – and I always admired her go-get-it attitude. Neither of us grew up with much money in our households, so an internalised need for financial independence was another strong bond that we shared. She was the solution-finder in any situation that we found ourselves in. Shoot forward a few decades, and Denise is in her fifties. She lost her job, then shortly afterward her husband also lost his job, and then tragically her mother passed away horrifically from Covid-19. This all happened while the world was in a state of turmoil and flux due to the global pandemic. After this series of life-changing events, Denise sunk into a deep depression. At times, she couldn't see the point of carrying on, so intense was her grief. Despite her strong religious faith and devotion to her son, her only child, she was broken. She couldn't see her way through.

As a friend, I did my best to rally around her, but social distancing was still very much in place, so phone calls and video messages were our only contact. When

I felt she was ready to hear it, I reminded her just how resilient she was and always had been. I talked about the time she moved from Wolverhampton to New York, alone, living in a challenging part of the Bronx; how she had tried to navigate the very difficult Green Card system and adapted to the fast-paced, foreign living in that city. Despite having very little work experience before leaving the UK, she managed to get hired in jobs that would eventually lead her to Wall Street, earning a very handsome salary. During those times, she was uncertain of how she would survive and what the consequences would be of her decisions, but she took a leap of faith. And she did it.

I reminded her about the many triumphs and difficulties she'd had to overcome on her personal journey. She was in an unimaginable situation through no fault of her own, but I knew that she had the power to take back the reins of her life, using the life lessons her previous trials had brought her. The resilience and determination that she has demonstrated throughout her life were still there – she just needed to take baby steps to walk her through the darkness and to remember who she was. And she did just that. She walked. On the really difficult days, she got up, got out and walked into the woods, seeking refuge in Mother Nature, while also seeking expert help, and finding people she could trust to be a good sounding board. The goal here for my dearest friend was not material, it was just to feel well enough to function and get back to coping with life without her mum.

CALL ON YOUR RESILIENCE-BUILDING PAST

When we're young, we tend not to intellectualise or analyse our decisions in the way that we might as adults – we just get on with life. But it can be helpful to reflect on the past and the moments when you feel you came up short, or had a really tough time but got back up and tried again. The more we reflect on these examples of resilience-building, the sooner we can see that they are integral to believing that you can get through life's challenges. It's never a smooth, linear path. Rather, it's an up-and-down roller-coaster ride with highs and lows – and stomach-churning surprise drops; but it is one that you know you can survive, and you can get off and stand on firm ground again when the dizzying part is over.

A resilience-building exercise

Make a note of your answers to the following:

1. Write down three times in your life when you've worked through a major challenge.
2. How did you feel, in each situation?
3. What did you do to work through it?
4. Who did you speak to, and where was the support?
5. What did those experiences teach you? Were they lessons that you take with you today?
6. How did those major challenges change you as a person?

BUILD A TOOLKIT

One of the most powerful tools you need in this world is the mental ability to flick a switch from potential panic to problem solving. Finding a coping strategy to get through difficult patches in the same way that sports people can is invaluable. Knowing you can do it – that you have that weapon in your mind's arsenal – will give you the confidence to change and adapt to new situations without freezing on the spot.

Competing in heptathlon taught me a lot about simple coping strategies when faced with tricky moments or disappointments. It took me a little while to embed them into my brain when the pressure was on during major championships. Eventually, however, I could use those trusted tools that had helped me in sport, and I needed to bring them into all areas of my life, not just in a sporting arena. The mind is a muscle – as important as the lungs, or the heart. It can unlock so many things, and I worked on my mind in the way that I would work on other parts of my body to give me the best chance of success. I'm sure my belief in this process is why I love watching and playing golf so much. That sport really challenges you to remain centred, and taking a full swing and trying to stay out of the rough is such a great life analogy. Picking the right club – when you've ended up in the crappy stuff and desperately need to get back on to the fairway – is what we are all trying to do. The mindset of good golfers is a lesson in focus and Zen.

One of the greatest struggles in heptathlon for me was working out how to move from event to event, leaving behind the emotional baggage of the previous competition in order to regain focus and move on to the next challenge. There should be minimal time spent on regret or disappointment; those moments of reflection need to happen away from the track and the emotion of the moment. Equally, any endorphins produced by a positive experience, such as a new personal best on your first throw of the javelin when you still have two more throws, is great, but you have to control the euphoria, otherwise you might lose focus and jeopardise the opportunity to throw further on the remaining throws. But how can you get your head in the right space?

I worked with a sports psychologist just after my surprise victory in the 1994 Commonwealth Games in Victoria, Canada, who taught me about visualisation: a key skill that you will see pop up in other chapters, because it is so important and yet so underused in daily life. These days people may refer to it as 'manifestation' – both are ways to cultivate positive thinking and adapt your mind away from negativity. I wanted to learn more about being mentally ready to win (a skill I didn't have before those games) and handling my emotions from event to event.

Like anything worth doing well, visualisation is a practice, helping you to learn and grow, and practice makes perfect. At the beginning, I found my mind wandering, a bit like when someone tells you to calm down when you're irate and the last thing you can do is be calm. Managing to still your mind isn't easy, especially in the cauldron of high-level sports, but it is essential in everyday life, to cope with the highs and lows of juggling work and a family, your home life or a new project or career challenge.

AN ATHLETE'S MINDSET MOMENT

I remember being at the 1996 Olympics, out of the medals in seventh place, and taking part in the penultimate event – the javelin. Sabina Braun from Germany, who had been the firm favourite but was not having her best competition, watched me throw a personal best after having seen how disappointing my other events had been at the championships. I moved up to the bronze-medal position and she said, 'How did you find that?' I told her that, at that moment, I was channelling what it would mean to me to turn my poor performance around. I had been visualising what I needed to *do* at that moment to improve my result.

The desire to *win* in that moment doesn't come into play, because it's about focusing on *one element* to centre your thoughts. Another example of this is when I've had an awful running session in training that's planned on my programme and I'm anticipating the pain; I don't look forward to it and my internal conversations are saying: *I hate this, I don't want to do it, I can't stand this session*. In this situation and with this mindset, the chances are it's not going to work out well.

Instead, affirming in your mind that: *The session's going to hurt, but I'm going to deal with each run as it comes and try to hit my target* is a much more positive approach. That's mental preparation for a session. It's difficult. But you're giving yourself an opportunity to be able to get the best out of the session, because your mind is focused on something *other* than the outcome of the pain. You're tapping into an energy system that is going to produce discomfort in the same way that marriage does. And you've just got to prepare yourself.

 think about resilience–building

Make a note of your answers to the following:

1. In what way could you 'throw with the other hand' to challenge yourself?
2. What might you notice, if you were to do this?
3. How would this feed into other parts of your work?
4. Do you have mental barriers stopping you from experimenting?
5. How can you change that?

ZOOMING IN

What worked for me when I needed to move on during a competition was a physical trigger, as I mentioned in Chapter 1. It needed to be something that could make me narrow my focus and *zoom in*. Once I completed one event, I would change my shoes for the next one, and that was the moment when I moved forward, only focusing on what was needed immediately – the emotions of the previous discipline parked for a future time. I had trained myself to maintain purpose with a sense that I was self-directing: staying in the moment. I would zoom in on what I needed to focus on: *I'm now a high jumper; I'm feeling light and springy.* I would replicate the thought with movement – either skipping or doing take-off drills that mirror what you do at take-off for that event. *I want to be bouncy, so I bounce.* I translated mentally what was needed physically, locking the movement and emotion needed *in that moment.*

Is there a physical anchor that you could use to help you transition from one state to another, zooming in on what you need to do or be at that particular moment – a swipe of lipstick before you walk into the office? Sipping from a certain water bottle before a post-workday run? A mantra in the mirror every morning? Think about these little self-coaching techniques that you could use to set or reset your focus.

ZOOMING OUT

Feeling emotional, angry or upset? That's your cue to *zoom out* of the situation a little bit. Distract yourself – take in something else. If you're having a bad day at work – distract yourself. Think about something else: what might you do later on, for example, a small thing to shift your attention elsewhere. Take yourself out of that feeling. Give yourself a mental break. This strategy (and zooming in) can be used in many areas of your life, not just in a sports setting. When they say that the lessons learned through sports are invaluable, I can vouch that it is true.

Here's an example: I had spent weeks preparing for a big speech in front of 1,500 sales employees and suppliers for a big company. In the weeks leading up to the conference the correspondence between myself and the team really intensified. Having constructed a good presentation, which I partly shared with the sales team, they were nevertheless showing signs of concern. They hadn't used a former athlete to deliver a keynote address before, and email exchanges got so much that I remember suggesting that if they didn't trust my ability, they were at liberty to get someone else to do it. Being assertive at that moment allowed me the opportunity to rehearse stress-free in the days leading up to my speech, instead of someone unintentionally chipping away at it.

On the actual day of the conference, I arrived and it was clear that the person I had been liaising with was still on tenterhooks, which in turn was spiking my adrenaline. Recognising this, I politely excused myself and spent a few minutes in the bathroom to clear my mind, calm myself and *zoom out* of the situation that was making me tense. Through finding my calm again, I was actively managing the situation, creating an environment conducive for me to feel in control. In the end I smashed it, and my presentation was well received.

Which zooming-out escape routes have you built for yourself during stressful moments? Can you take a five-minute stroll outside the office between meetings? Can you call a friend and plan a fun weekend meet-up? Anything you can do that helps you to think better and beyond the stressful situation you are in will help you to zoom out and see the bigger picture.

EXPLAINING MANSPLAINING

As a woman in sport or any other male-dominated indus-try, you might have to hold a certain amount of masculine energy. What do I mean by that? These are competitive spaces, and whether we like it or not, being slightly thick-skinned, assertive and self-confident will help to keep you in the game. This can be hard, and you might come up against criticism, especially if you're competing with men for jobs, promotions or board positions, for example. In my experience in sport, women have adapted to the demands of training, putting in as long hours and as much effort as our male counterparts – pushing our body, and breaking it down to rebuild it – we are not soft and fragile people that can't hack it. Sport aside, women get through pregnancy, childbirth and nursing a baby (in many countries where there is no sophisticated equipment and machinery or medical intervention, they just have to get on with it), and if that's not showing power and resilience, I don't know what is.

The question has been: is resilience integral to adapting? Women need to ask themselves: *What does it take right now? What do I need right now? How do I forget my femininity, for a moment?* I'm an advocate of acting like a woman and thinking like a man when it comes to getting what you need and not being apologetic about it. Adapt to be as forthright and secure in yourself as the man competing for a promotion next to you would be. And yes, fake it till you own it, if you must, for a while.

STAND UP TO THE CHALLENGES
OF INTERSECTIONALITY

Building tools to withstand the journey of womanhood, and particularly the daily battle against prejudice based on race and gender or sexuality, is one of the biggest calls on your resilience and adaptability. In the book *Slay in Your Lane* by Yomi Adegoke and Elizabeth Uviebinené, they feature a quote by the filmmaker Destiny Ekaragha, from an interview she did in the *Guardian* in 2014:

> I'm not just black, I am a woman, so there are two glass ceilings I have to break every time I open my mouth. But if I wake up in the morning and think, *Oh my God, I've got two ceilings I have to smash today*, that's no way to live.

I've felt this; I'm sure many of you have, too, be it with a combination of gender, race, class or sexuality.

The intersectional layers that women of colour carry are heavy. Ask the majority of black women in this country, and at some point in their young lives, they will have been told by a parent that they have to work twice as hard as white people to gain recognition for what they do. And once they do, there's a feeling that there is not much room for mistakes or underperforming. Worse still, they often feel that they can't bring their authentic self into the roles they occupy. The responsibility to shine weighs far heavier than for our white female counterparts even though, having spoken to many white women in senior management roles, their grievances are mirrored from a gender-balance lens. The feeling of: *I must not fail when I've been given this opportunity, otherwise I might not get another chance for a while* rings true for all women – but it is compounded further when ethnicity is also in play.

I've had to deal with extremely jarring microaggressions, whereas others have had experiences of overt racism and discrimination. Their stories of inequality and what it feels like to be a black woman in the UK in many industries where we are vastly underrepresented and often the only black woman in the room, show incredible resilience and adaptability. Becoming a chameleon in order to blend in is OK if you have intentionally set out to do so with the understanding that these are your rules of engagement while you assess your environment. Be in charge of who you want to be and how you want to be seen; adapt in a way that feels right for you.

Since retiring from athletics, I've been given a handful of broadcasting opportunities outside sport. When I started out in TV, I co-hosted my own show for four years and dabbled in a few one-off series, but I never had a sense that there was room for growth or progression. It could have been that I wasn't good enough as a presenter, but when I look back at that period between 2013 and 2020, I realise that there were fewer women of colour on screen as presenters, actors, or in commercials compared with how the landscape looks now. Talented individuals were penned in, incapable of smashing that glass ceiling, because of how they looked. Finally, things are starting to change, and there are adaptations on a huge societal scale.

How to get what you deserve

- Find allies or a network that help to strengthen your resolve. Having someone to champion you is invaluable.
- Stand up for yourself – thoughtfully, by reading the room. Thinking that you can walk into a new space and immediately start putting the world to rights will not only make you very unpopular but it may also get you sacked. Your peers might be comfortable with the status quo. How hard can, or should, one push for change in this situation? The response to this will vary depending on how, and where, you perceive your position of influence.

- Being good at your job isn't the only prerequisite: women who have landed senior roles have shown passion and consistency to get to where they are.
- Look for inspiration. Seeing other black women ahead of me competing in track and field events both domestically and internationally gave me confidence that there would be a place for me if I was good enough.
- Sports is often, thankfully, an outlier of discrimination. You are not going to be judged by where you were educated, your accent, or your skin colour, if you're the best. However, at the height of my career as an Olympic gold medallist, the opportunity to maximise my exposure was not available to me. The brand I was sponsored by had no marketing strategy for me – the focus on male sports stars was the only currency in that space. I was told by my agent at the time that he was unable to get a front cover for me on any fashion or beauty publication because I was *not relatable*. A sign of the times perhaps, but I was shocked and hurt.

GET A GOOD WORK ETHIC

You are a product of what you see. You look to your parents, or parent, and tend to follow their lead. If they don't have much money, you see that they have to keep working. You learn those lessons from a young age, and they become deeply embedded in your sense of self and what the future will look like for you. I'm a product of *you've got to work hard.* There won't be too many Black homes or homes of people descending from the African diaspora, Caribbean or Asian, that will not have been told at some point: *You have to work bloody hard as an immigrant. You've got to work hard because you are the minority.* And therefore, to be seen, you've got to push ahead and you've got to work hard. You've got to get the grades and you've got to hit the targets, and you've got to excel.

In terms of getting back up after dealing with failure, I would say that what kept me going was having pride in myself. When you have pride, you keep going. You don't stay in that pit of doom. And that's what I saw my mum doing: she wanted to do better. She had setbacks, but she did keep going. And I can only imagine that is because she had a sense of pride. Isn't that what drives us all? I think there is an innate sense of pride that we have, but when we don't tap into it and understand why we get up in the morning, why we go to work, why we do whatever we do – that's when we falter.

Perhaps some people give up, but perhaps that's because they haven't seen that resilience piece elsewhere in their environment. Some people can't see a roadmap out of difficult situations; they can't access the drive within them, or they have limited self-esteem. I feel a sense of responsibility to give my best, and that has only increased with the direction in which my life has taken me. I want to max out on spaces that I can penetrate, as a source of gratitude for how far I've come and who I might inspire in the process. I guess my strong work ethic is partly due to being an only child. So much is wrapped up in that because I know that I am my mum's legacy.

Therefore, if you're feeling marginalised in your working environment, don't get angry, get smart. Think of it as an 800-metre race: you know it's going to hurt; you have done the hard yards of preparation to be on that start line; you have to display good pace judgement, sit in tight and prepare for the sprint finish. Your goal is completing the distance despite the lactic pain and feeling that you want to give up. The rewards will be that by lasting the distance you will inspire others to have a go. The pursuit of change is worth it in the long run.

MAINTAIN A MARRIAGE

When we talk about resilience, perhaps it's our careers or hobbies that first spring to mind. But resilience can be built across all the sectors of our lives, including our relationships. I've been married for seventeen years. It's been a roller coaster, as you'd expect of most marriages, but it's the lessons that stay with me more than the arguments or the upsets. When you're building a marriage, each partner is trying to be their own person while nurturing the relationship with one another. Plus, if children come along, you're also building a family life and adapting to various difficult family situations, with more individuals needing your time, love, energy, direction, support and care.

I think the recipe for a successful marriage is to keep the scales balanced between togetherness and making sure that you can maintain harmony in your own head and heart. The scales will tip at various points, and are never static, and you will be adapting to what everyone needs in the family, or in your career, at any particular time. Life is busy, and stressors come in many forms. Before you know it, your life is composed of routines, and you are just trying to get through the week instead of refuelling your passion and exploring new adventures – and you can forget why you chose to be with one another.

It's really been good between me and Steve when we

consciously invest time in each other. We write it down and schedule it. Because otherwise it's all too easy to take each other for granted and have an expectation that quality time is just going to happen. The reality is, when you're busy, tired or stressed, it doesn't, does it? Putting each other in your diaries, and scheduling a date, is key to staying resilient as a couple. If you don't have the same interests, one of you will have to adapt and take the ego out of the equation, and then do something the other partner enjoys – but the next time, it will be the other one who makes the compromise. Who knows, you might even enjoy or learn something new when you're taking date ideas in turn?

Steve and I came very late to the power of walking together, and how side-by-side dialogue can actually make for fruitful engagement. I say late, it's something we should really have learned much earlier in our marriage to prevent the escalation of problems. We are both strong characters with different conflict styles. I mentioned in the opening chapter how your childhood baggage can quickly creep into your most intimate relationships and impact them greatly if you're not careful, and this was true of us. Since writing this book, I've been forced to examine just what personality types really look like and how they clash as a result of these conflict styles. But for us, walking and talking together has become a lifeline. Before learning to do that, we'd always be trying to sort things out on the hoof, while doing breakfast or preparing for the school run, not giving each other our full attention because our days were crammed from top to bottom. But taking time to properly listen to each other is so important – rather than half-listening – so that you can pick up the essence of what the other person is saying without distractions. When walking in nature where it's calm, we can be attentive and listen properly to each other, which isn't always achievable at home. This has been a big plus for us, and is the essence of adaptability.

Throw away the heaviness

- What can be helpful when you hit a rocky patch in an intimate partnership is to perform like a shot-putter: that is, to hold on to the issue briefly and then throw it away, because holding on to that heavy weight for too long is uncomfortable.
- You need good technical knowledge and speed across the circle, then you need to let that weight go!
- Understand the dynamics of your relationship, and quickly move into solution-finding ideas, such

as a date night or finding a fun activity. Change the interaction and make time for each other, letting go of your egos.

- It doesn't matter who makes the first move to finding a resolution as long as you get to a positive place.
- Speaking to a professional coach can be very valuable.
- Ask yourselves important questions such as: 'How are we doing?' 'How are we doing as a family?' Check in to know whether you are both on the same page: 'What could we do better right now?'
- We tend to think that communication should just happen organically, but we have many distractions these days, so it is necessary that you are clearer about what you need.

LESS ROMANCE, MORE RESILIENCE

We are a blended family with cultural differences and experiences, multiple kids and two working parents, so it takes mental agility. It requires both people adapting. As a parent, the race is against time and how you divide it up: social activities, work, partners, kids, the dog! After years of caregiving and career making, I have definitely felt mental burnout, but my reservoir runs deep (too much resilience perhaps) and sometimes I haven't given into my gut when it was screaming out: 'Something has got to change!' I think I'm normal in that respect. Typically, when raising a family or being a caregiver and juggling work commitments, we women often neglect ourselves.

I am a product of my upbringing: raised in a clean and tidy home, I don't like to go to bed with a messy kitchen, because I don't like to walk down and see things in the sink first thing in the morning. My mum didn't either; when I was growing up, however tired she was, she did the clearing up. Our house was small with no dishwasher, so she'd be standing up, cleaning everything after a long day at work. But she did it, and now I do it, too. It's non-negotiable, because it makes me feel better at the start of the new day; however, no one else cares in the same way that I do. And it drives me mad.

I got some good insights on how to get a grip on what changes needed to happen at my house after a chance encounter with a fabulous woman with whom I had been thrown together at a very intimate dinner of twelve females, all representing different industries. We got chatting, struck a rapport, laughed, and I found myself almost oversharing, not knowing where it was all coming from. I told her about my mum living in the Midlands, two hours' drive from me, and the guilt I feel about this separation, because if something happened to her, it's a journey for me to get there. I had tried to get her to move nearer to me, but she didn't want to. She's stubborn and independent (good for her), but this was another demand on my emotional well-being. As my innermost concerns about my home life – my responsibilities as a woman, wife, mother and daughter – started to emerge, my confidante said, 'You need to read a book by Eve Rodsky, called *Fair Play: Share the mental load, rebalance your relationship and transform your life*'. And she actually sent it to me from America, where she lives.

When the book landed on my doorstep a little while later, I started reading it and it was as if someone had written it just for me. It felt like the author was saying: *Dear Denise, this is what you've been feeling and I know why you've been feeling this.* The author wrote about the invisible jobs that women do that tend not to get noticed or appreciated, and she encourages the reader to make a list of all the chores they did for their family with no recognition.

I was staggered by my list. It just went on and on. At last, I could see that it's not just me and my mind feeling that I'm being pulled in so many different directions – I really was! The organisation, diary-keeping, follow-up emails, contact with the schools, the additional SENCO (special educational needs and disabilities coordinator) stuff I have to do, the appointments – and the list goes on. I talked to Steve about it, asking him, 'Does this look fair?' He briefly acknowledged what I was saying, and there was a temporary change where he did more, but then it went back to how it always had been.

I've had two decades of this parenting life, and it all seemed rosy in the beginning, being a working mum, but it takes its toll after a while if you're not getting the support and understanding that you need. But too often, when we ask for help, it's framed as complaining or nagging, isn't it? Well, if I could burn any word, it would be 'nag'. I hate that word with a passion, it's so demeaning, because so-called 'nagging' is just asking for help, it's someone telling you 'I'm struggling, I need help.' Sometimes we women can be a little too resilient for our own good, can't we?

Resilience in marriage

Make a note of your answers to the following:

1. If you're married or in a long-term relationship, what do you find hardest about it?
2. How do you deal with conflict?
3. What allowances do you make for your partner?
4. Do you have clear boundaries in certain areas?
5. What one thing would improve your relationship?
6. How would you like your life to look in ten years' time?
7. If you could ask your partner to change three things, what would they be?

At home, you might feel as if it's always you who steps up when you have a difficult situation or crisis, and that requires clarity of thought. There are only so many hours in a day, and too often we're stuck in that mode of: *OK, that needs doing – I've got only so many hours to fit that in, I've got to prepare the bag for tomorrow, wash the kit*, and so on. You're constantly on. And that's the state I've been in for a while: constantly on, and I consciously had to take myself off and switch to a mode of: *I am going to go into town and I'm going to watch something at the theatre. Everyone will be fine and I'll be able to switch off, come back refreshed, renewed, and ready for another day.*

To keep myself feeling good, I need to step away from the pressure of family life, and give myself a few hours of pure self-indulgence, of friendship and laughter. Those breaks are how I tap back into myself and regenerate. With my female friends there are natural common spaces. We have moved through having babies, a child at school having issues, processing changes in our marriages, ageing parents and tricky careers. We're good at talking about those things and finding comfort and solace in one another, or a sense of understanding about why we need to share in that way. Always make time for yourself, please – you have more than earned it.

MORPHING INTO A MOTHER

No matter whether your child was planned or not, the moment you see those two lines appear on your pregnancy test, well, it really is a moment. I had never contemplated what type of mother I would like to be, so there was an initial: *Oh fuck! How is this going to impact my career?* I had spent all my childhood dreaming of, and working towards, my title as an Olympian, but I hadn't thought about if and when motherhood would come into it.

Then other questions followed: *How will my body adapt and recover? Will I be able to perform to the level I want to again?* Attempting to combine motherhood and sport felt like mixing oil and water. I joked in a recent podcast with Anna Whitehouse that becoming a mother as an Olympic champion wasn't on the performance pathway – according to my then coach and mentor. But it wasn't a joke; it was true. I was about to embark on a journey for which I hadn't trained, because there is no way to train for motherhood. You cannot know for sure what type of mother you'll become until you meet your baby and start that journey together. This becomes a real adapting piece of life's puzzle: you identify the baby's needs, you tend to them, you hopefully continue to identify some of your own needs, ask for – and accept – support. But I wouldn't know this until I met my first child, Lauryn. I was unprepared for motherhood, and I was also unprepared for being a pregnant athlete.

There was no question in my mind, however, that I would return to being a professional sportswoman, despite the unhelpful undertones that circulated when I announced that I was pregnant. Many of the interviews I remember giving at the time centred on whether I would be as focused, determined, physically capable or as motivated once I had a child. I questioned these things myself, too. Yes, I was an Olympic champion, but what would it mean when I added the new layer of motherhood? I didn't believe the two had to be mutually exclusive. Why would motherhood alter my character, professionalism or commitment?

How do you handle big changes?

When I got pregnant the first time, I was filled with questions and was desperate for answers – and some took a long time for me to work out. It's the same with any big life change. How do you react to new information? Have a think about your answers to the questions below so that you can prepare yourself better for your next big adaptation.

1. When a big change is happening, do you immediately panic or become fretful?
2. Do you take your time to process and start figuring out a plan of action?
3. Who is, or are, the go-to individuals to share new information and help you order your thoughts?

4. Are you volatile or an avoidant? Do you refuse to shy away from making your point and tend to be more confronting than retreating? Or do you deal with conflict by moving into your own time and space to deal with the situation, writing it down or perhaps waiting for someone else to raise the subject?

5. Do you understand that situations adapt and evolve and that there are often opportunities to reopen doors that feel as if they've been closed? Have you embraced the excitement and opportunity in adapting to change?

FORTITUDE FOR THE FAMILY

Building resilience should also be about building resilience in your network or family. When my children have to fend for themselves, or the household has to spend a few days without me, they have to make a bit more effort to be helpful. Because when I'm there, there's an assumption that I'll do all the washing, go around the rooms getting everything ready and leave instructions or requests for people to put their washing in this place or that. Invariably, if it doesn't get done, I'm going to be the one taking care of it. And once you do it a couple of times, any intentions that you had for everyone to take responsibility and ownership has completely gone. You are, therefore, back to square one where you're running around doing everything and complaining about the fact that you're doing it. And so, when I get some time away and say, 'No, I'm going', they just have to get it done themselves.

Is it just a societal expectation that mothers will do the kids and home that makes us worry? We are the diary-planners, the fixers, the coordinators. I don't know whether it's all society, or whether it's also that the maternal female feels naturally led to run the home in this way. Either way, we haven't broken away from what society expected fifty years ago in terms of women and home. But we've just added more to our plates, because we want to be astronauts, CEOs and Olympic champions as well. You are not alone. Most women feel this at some point and need to work with the people they share a home with to be better. Added to this, today most women *need* to work to provide for the family and/or pay for the mortgage, whether alone or in a relationship.

Build resilience as a mother

Make a note of your answers to the following:

1. What do you find hardest in motherhood?
2. What are you good at?
3. How do you keep going when things feel tough?
4. Who can you lean on for support?
5. When have you been the most resilient as a mum?

I learned so much about resilience through my athletics training, and yet I haven't always seen it translate into my parenting. I have definitely found parenting to be the greatest challenge of my life. I try to eliminate negativity – getting angry, snapping – but I'm not always successful. When the pressures are high and I haven't got maximum compliance, that's when I struggle. It's normal, and they're kids not wired to be robotic. They need challenges, and as they get older to explore their boundaries. They need to be allowed to fail or, at least, to work out how to overcome the problem, which isn't the mentality of a high-achieving parent. All too often the instinct is to fix, solve the problem and facilitate everything, and to impart all your knowledge and experience into their tiny minds. With a lot of my recent self-examination, I realise that my own childhood experience was about that: a little independence. Society has moved on a lot in the past forty years with the advancement in technology, with working hours that are longer, and more emphasis on parents taking on a more engaged approach in schooling than ever before.

The times are different, parents are stretched, and I have experienced the expectations to be a super-parent, available for everything, and it's too much at times. The reality is that you can't, and you mustn't feel guilty about not doing it all. It's OK not to be present at every play, every sports day or every music recital. My mum didn't come to any of my sports days during my childhood because she had to work, and it didn't hamper me becoming an Olympic champion. In fact, I imagine it could have fuelled me, because it was a journey that I owned, and it was not about pleasing anyone other than myself.

Every household is different, however. What is working and easy to implement in one home can be vastly different from another. The dynamics are different, the personalities of the individuals within it are different, and yet we get drawn into thinking and behaving with a herd mentality. Stop. Adapt your family life into what *your* family wants and needs. Stop comparing yourself. Lean into what you believe and what you'd like to accomplish as a parent; think about how you're going to do it and how you're going to evolve. Adapting to societal expectations will only make you all miserable.

The ground around parenting is always shifting, so we need to be on our toes as parents, always evolving better ways to communicate with Gen Z, who don't respond well to dated methods of parenting, and remembering that every child is different. Being consistent and reassuring with your kids as to why you take certain actions while being clear on your boundaries will hopefully serve you and your family well in the long run.

STAY STRONG IN A BLENDED FAMILY

I left Patrick, Lauryn's father, when she was 18 months old. He was a really lovely guy and a great dad, but I couldn't see a future with him in my life. It was a scary decision to make, and I dreaded what the fallout would be. It would have seemed easier perhaps to just stay in the relationship and not rock the boat, but I had tried – even moving partially to Belgium to be with him there – but ultimately, for all of us, it was best to end things. It was hard raising a baby alone in London. And yet, I weathered the storm. I met and married my now husband when Lauryn was four and a half. When she was about six, she asked me if she could call Steve daddy and even though I knew that Patrick would find it hard, I also know it was what Lauryn needed in order to feel a sense of belonging with her little brother in tow. The adults would have to adapt. And, to be fair to Patrick, he did adapt slowly, and allowed us to present a united front for her sake, adapting his emotions to help with hers. Thankfully, we all weathered the choppy waters and maintained friendly and civil relationships.

I would say to anyone in a similar circumstance, if you put the child's best interest at the centre of everything, you will get to a healthy place – it just takes time and a willingness to adapt to your new familial situation. The other thing I would say about adapting to be a blended family is to do your homework. I could have done a bit more research into kids' emotions around this topic instead of assuming that I had a grip on other people's positions, feelings, expectations or opinions. Read lots, talk to friends who have been through similar things, and ask yourself lots of questions about how you want the changing family dynamic to work. What would you like to achieve? What is the goal? How are we going to achieve it? What do we need to put into place to ensure that everyone can be united for the child and go in the right direction? Prolonged feelings of resentment are costly for children and adults. It was uncharted territory for me, and these were the key things I learned that I would do differently and that would have made me feel more resilient in those changing times.

ADAPT TO LIFE WITH TEENAGERS

I might be an experienced parent, but one thing is for sure: adapting to the teenage years is difficult every time. Particularly as a mother, I feel we are always six months behind in the mental preparation it takes to adapt your emotions to your tweens' demand for more independence. It feels as if their cutting of the apron strings happens overnight and you've been caught off guard. You resist because you're not quite ready even though they claim that they are! This transition for parents would be so much easier if we purposefully gave our little people more independence sooner, so how do we do that?

- Simple tasks, where they are stretched out of their comfort zone, making them more hands-on with tasks around the home.
- Taking them off their tablets or devices when travelling so that they get a better sense of direction and familiarity about different environments. This is not only an exercise for them, but it is also reassuring

for you that you have street-smart kids that learn to spot danger as they prepare for adulthood.

- I was a state-school child of the 1970s and 1980s, so walking to school and independently mobilising myself was the norm. The challenge is to give them enough situations where they feel uncertain but gain confidence for doing the task set for them by you.
- This is why I love music, sport and drama for children: where they have a little bit of concern about how well they will do, but they come through it.

My son Kane had stage fright when he was in year 4. I sat there and wanted to scoop him up and take him away from the glaring eyes of a hundred parents watching him dry up as he was unable to deliver his lines. His drama teacher, Jane Trainer, found me after the show and suggested that I do more work with him to help with his fear of performing in front of people. By year 8, after much perseverance, he got 99 per cent in his speech and drama performance, reciting plays and performing them, and later he was a drama scholar at his secondary school. Our children must experience disappointments and failure to eventually successfully fly the nest.

I'm late to the letting-go part of kids growing up; I'm always looking for little things to helicopter about: are they happy; are they safe? While looking for little clues as to what they're thinking, I'm sometimes so busy searching that I miss the big clues that they're moving on. We need to adapt to them growing up, while teaching them to adapt to the world in which they will find themselves fully submerged before anyone knows it. I want my kids to experience challenges for their betterment – not hardship because I worry; they don't have the soft skills to deal with life's changes and experience helps children to learn them.

I think it is our parental duty to start early when it comes to teaching independence, not that I've always got it right. I have encouraged independence with my three oldest between the ages of three and seven, and then, without fully realising it, I have set up mini blockages to try to halt them moving on after that. It's hard for a parent to watch their kids grow up. Now, I'm watching Troy, my five-year-old, struggling to do up the buttons on his first shirt, and being desperate to intervene, but I'm trying to take a step back. They've got to keep going alone, and they've got to feel their progress, which will make them feel capable and proud. Yes, I could rush in every morning and do up his buttons for him, but we need to let our kids step out of their comfort zone in these small ways. I wish I had let all my kids do more for themselves sooner. A chore, a task, sitting in their uncomfortable feelings and acquiring the personal skill to work through them. I do believe my independence as a child was the making of me.

Sometimes, little restrictions and challenges can help our children to learn to be adaptable in the real world. During Covid-19, when I could only get a food shop once a week, I rationed the kids' treats, putting them in individual boxes. They had to learn to control themselves, not to stuff it all in on one day, and they had to learn to barter with each other to get what they fancied. If one of them wanted an extra packet of crisps, and the other person wanted more chocolate, they'd have to work it out. By no means would they get anything else until the seven days were up, and I held strong on that. They worked it out.

Once they get to the teenage years, if they haven't experienced any sort of pushback, they'll struggle with the real trials and restrictions of navigating adult life. They haven't had to deal with any of my early struggles, they haven't experienced any deprivation so far in their lives, so I do what I can in my quest to keep them as humble and resilient as possible – striking a balance between teaching them values and a work ethic, while allowing them to live a life easier than mine was, which I feel grateful to be able to give them.

WHEN A BIG CHANGE HITS THE FAMILY UNIT

Kane was the youngest in the family, and when he was ten years old, I got pregnant aged forty-seven, and Troy came along. Obviously, Kane was a little taken aback: 'Oh, I'm not the baby any more,' but he quickly got over it when he realised that he didn't actually *like* being the baby, having to go to bed the earliest and getting too much parental attention. I explained to all the kids that our world would change a bit when I was pregnant and beyond, and I was very clear about my intentions: what I needed to do, and what they needed to do to step up a little bit, in terms of helping around the house and doing a bit more for themselves. With any change to the family dynamic, I've worked out that it's best to be upfront about the situation. Don't treat kids as if they are idiots, because they're not, they are very alert to what is going on around them and more resilient than you might think. If you try to hide things, they'll imagine the worst. We can be so fearful about telling kids about change, and we think we're protecting them, but it's all about how you share information. When you're discussing the adaptations that your family is making, be excited, honest and positive. Be age appropriate – don't overburden them. They are listening by osmosis, soaking in your attitude, so show strength and they'll feel strong standing beside you.

ADAPT YOUR LIFE AROUND YOUR NEURODIVERGENT CHILDREN

When you have high-functioning, neurodivergent children, sometimes the diagnosis isn't conclusive (meaning that there is no evidence for medication), but how you live with or deal with them as individuals has to be modified, and it takes great resilience from everyone – the child, the parents and the siblings – to do so. If you have no experience or specialist training, as we often don't as parents, you can be really late to understanding what it takes and the skill sets you need to adapt to service your children better – and save your own sanity. I've spent many years frustrated, feeling as if I were a bad parent for not staying calm when confronted by rudeness from a couple of my children in their formative years, behaviours that were challenging and beyond what one would consider acceptable teenage angst.

Having gone through the child-psychologist process and SENCO evaluations a couple of times, I have a greater awareness and acceptance of any shortcomings that I may have had in my early years of parenting and have found the adaptability that it takes to let go, seek support and realise that you won't get it right all the time. Be strong in trusting your gut instinct when you know that a certain reaction or behaviour isn't quite right, and ask for advice and support as early as possible. Identification methods in schools have evolved so much, and I am truly grateful to the teachers who have guided and supported me, particularly over the last decade when I have been crying, at my wits' end, not knowing what to do. I can recall many occasions sitting in a school office realising that a conversation was alluding to another one of my children showing signs of being autism-spectrum disorder (ASD). The first fear as a parent is the life label that will follow your child, because, as a parent, all you want to do is protect. This is swiftly followed by the second fear of how you can best support their needs – and believe me, this is not a cheap process! If ever you need to be resilient as a mum, it's in the middle of all that. One of my current school-mum friends commented to me recently that people don't realise just how difficult it can be having a child with ASD.

I've had to tap into my patience reservoir as a parent of neurodivergent kids. As you can imagine, I want things done yesterday, but with a child who is neurodivergent that does not work: they need time to adjust situationally; they need to be made aware of what's coming – they don't tend to like surprises, so being spontaneous doesn't always work out well. I've had to learn, and in turn teach. I've had to make extremely difficult choices and decisions that have resulted in a big change within my family set-up to give the best outcomes for all my children. Showing love comes in many forms, some of which are hard for others to comprehend, but as a mother you need to trust your gut feeling, knowing that it comes from the best intentions. Fear of being judged has kept me awake at night, but I always circle back to what's best for my child. What gives them the best opportunity to thrive: that's what keeps me strong.

GET A WINNING MINDSET

When I look back on everything I wanted to include in this chapter about resilience and adaptability, I think about my old coach, Charles. He had this idea that you needed to be regularly getting outside your comfort zone and testing your skills. If I was going through a moment of thinking that I couldn't do something, he would suggest an exercise such as throwing the javelin with my non-dominant hand. When you're told to do something like that, your first thought is: *There's no way I can do that! I can't throw with the other hand. That's not going to work.* And then, when I managed to do it, I would then return to the original challenge feeling more positive and hopeful.

It was about changing my attitude. Dealing with resistance, which is an energy-sapping response. Resistance is a negative. Charles would throw me a curveball challenge that would require me to open my mind and give it a go. It would feel weird, and perhaps I would fall over or hit the back of my head with a javelin or just not perform the way I would have imagined or would have liked to, but if I then do it another five times, I might get the hang of it and feel OK. Resilience.

I'm sure there is no one, whether it's in business or elsewhere, who has not been thrown a curveball, or needed to change direction. In order to succeed, we will need to try new things, take risks, challenge ourselves, hire people, fire people, make mistakes, pick ourselves up and move on. People have gone bankrupt in order to grow. The challenge, in terms of growth, is not to make the same mistake again. It is a learning tool, and for my family and me throwing with the non-dominant hand was about: *Are you ready to be shocked in a new way? Are you ready to do something different? And what's your attitude to that?*

It was also about preparing, because this is in training, but when you're competing it's possible that something could happen – or be thrown at you – that is unexpected. How will you deal with that? Perhaps it's a thunderstorm in the middle of a competition: you're doing really well and you are about to break your own personal record and then the clouds come over, the rain's falling down. You think: *Oh, my goodness, why is this happening to me now?* You then steady yourself and think: *How can I adapt?* You will think about the fact that the surface is now wet, so you're going to have to move differently. But you can't let it consume you to the point that you assume you're going to fail. You've got to be prepared for these curveballs.

Something else we used to do when training was to engineer sleep deprivation to test our ability to deal with jet lag. If you don't know how to deal with jet lag, or know how many days it might take you to get over it – or if you're not used to waking up at the crack of dawn – you're not going to be ready to compete. But if you do it a few times, learn about how you cope in these different scenarios and what you need to do to adapt, you will be better prepared. Again, it's about switching it up and forcing yourself to engage in a challenge when it's not actually required of you. Test your adaptability, test your limits, then get full marks for resilience.

Five ways to become more resilient

1. Don't shy away from a challenge: face it head-on.
2. Know that every successful person has failed more times than they have succeeded.
3. It takes a strong work ethic to succeed in life. Be prepared to put in the hours.

4. Resilience within relationships (marriage/as a mother) is much harder to build than it is within your career. It's worth it, though.

5. Challenge yourself by trying something well outside your comfort zone. By doing this, the zone stretches out and you become even more capable.

CHAPTER 3

Plan for Success

No matter who you are, no matter what you
did, no matter where you've come from, you
can always change, become a better version
of yourself.

MADONNA

What does success look like for you? I knew what that meant
when talking about targets for my sport, but what does it look
like for your life? Are you travelling a path that brings you joy?
When was the last time you stopped to evaluate where you
are and how you feel? When was the last time you felt you'd
achieved something? Too often in life we focus on what we
haven't done well, not stopping for a minute to take stock of

what we've done successfully and being proud of that. But the more we reflect on our winning and losing situations, the more we'll be able to adapt our life to plan for future success. And being successful takes physical and mental work.

Let's take running the London Marathon, as an example. You don't just get up one day and run 26.2 miles. You apply for your place, select the best running shoes and training programme for you, scheduling it around your other responsibilities. You may have set a target for the money you'd like to raise for your particular charity, too. Alongside training and fundraising, you're looking at your nutrition and sleep, preparing for the day. It's a real process.

Planning for success, therefore, starts by looking at what it is that you'd like to achieve. I like to call this your target. You might like to visualise an archery board with several circles; you're aiming for the central circle, but anywhere on that board is a hit. If you don't hit that central target, you still know you're aiming in the right direction and you've landed somewhere on that board, which means that you're on the right track.

It then requires a plan of action. You'll need to make sure your mindset is prepared for success; you can't be going into this thinking that it might not happen. You need to believe it will happen – and then look at what you need to do, right now, to kickstart the journey. A good place to start is by answering these questions:

1. What would you like to achieve? What makes you happy?
2. Is success related to happiness?
3. What are you willing to sacrifice for success?

When dealing with some of our closest relationships, such as partnerships, marriage or family, we don't always start with a to-do list or checklist of how we want to coexist. We don't always plan the hell out of it to ensure a happy existence, but we probably should. Now I'm going to share some stories that will give you some ideas about my own journey towards success, including what I was willing to sacrifice along the way and some of the key components of my success; for example: having a support network and adapting a game plan that wasn't working; the first taste of success; dealing with obstacles; and reaching the pinnacle of my chosen sport. I wouldn't have won gold without having a plan and being willing to adapt it when the path in front of me changed.

WHAT ARE YOU WILLING TO SACRIFICE FOR SUCCESS?

Planning for success is about willpower, preparation, feedback, analysis, being honest with yourself about your goals – and if you can achieve them – and finding it within you to change your behaviour when it is needed. As an athlete, this was second nature to me, and I easily adapted my life to commit fully to the behaviour changes I needed going from a teenage hopeful to a burgeoning athlete with huge potential, and then to a world leader in the field. Because of the clarity of my vision, making hard decisions for my own betterment came instinctively to me – such as leaving my hometown, club and the tutelage of the coach that took me to Olympic bronze – in pursuit of a more performance-driven environment.

Building better habits needs to become second nature. Once you're clear about your target, you'll need to hone in on the path that will take you there. Once on that path, you may well notice people and events that are no longer relevant/useful/beneficial dropping away; those things that used to feel important to you are no longer, as you become razor-focused on your target.

A visualisation for success

1. Think about what you're willing to sacrifice for your goal. This might require a deep visualisation into how determined you are to succeed. Once

you're clear on this, it becomes easier to let go of anything – or anyone – that will hold you back.

2. Close your eyes and take a deep breath in through your nose, letting it out loudly through your mouth.

3. Repeat three times.

4. Let your shoulders drop.

5. Relax into the seat you're sitting in or the bed you're lying on.

6. Now, go on a journey in your mind to that point, in the future, when you hit the centre of your target: the ultimate win.

7. How does it feel to be there?

8. What can you hear, smell, see, taste?

9. Spend some time in this moment, imagining that it's happening right now.

10. Who or what is trying to pull on your attention or distract you?

11. Imagine it dropping away.

NO (WO)MAN IS AN ISLAND

One of the most crucial elements in a plan for success is having a good group around you. The base layer of your support network may be at home (your parents when you're younger, or a partner when you're older), but what do you need outside of this? Think about your plan for success. Who is going to appear on your journey, to give you a leg-up? Get really clear on what support you're going to need, and start approaching those people to see if they will be willing to back you. If you don't ask, you don't get. Yes, this involves a level of courage, but if you really want to move forward, you're going to need to push yourself out of your comfort zone regularly. If they say no, ask someone else. Keep going until you start to create a cosy support group around you that will back you all the way. None of us do it alone, we all need our people to be there on the sidelines, keeping us going towards the finish line. We all need supporters, a cheerleader, to propel us on when we don't feel that we can continue.

My first mentor was very performance oriented and very clear in expectations about what it takes, which made him an effective mentor, because his advice and encouragement wasn't based on someone who was just happy that I was doing well. No, it was more on the lines of: how much do you give? Do you understand what it takes, and are you prepared to give that mentally and that daily dedication to the course? There's a really big difference between, for me, high performance and the level that I entered in 1994, as a Commonwealth champion. That still felt like the infancy. It didn't feel like it at the time, because I obviously didn't know what I would go on to do, but I was still on rung five of a hundred steps, if you like. What I had in those early years was a wide support network around me; and this is the most important part of planning for success: working out who you need around you to help make it happen. You can't do it on your own.

 How to deal with imposter syndrome

Make a note of your answers to the following:

1. What you have achieved towards your target, to date.
2. Note the failures you've overcome.
3. Reflect on any positive feedback you've been given about your past performance in your field.
4. Imagine that you have already achieved the greatest success and you're basking in it.
5. Write a sentence – in the first-person, present tense – about who you are, now that you have this success (for example, I am a gold Olympic champion, a mother, a champion for women's rights).

BACK YOURSELF

I remember going to a dinner in Birmingham in 1995, and sitting with seven local businessmen from the Midlands region. We got chatting about my hopes and goals of making it to the 1996 Olympics, which were only a year away. I talked about the challenges and what it would take to get there, and I boldly *suggested* that it would be incredible if they each gave me £1,000 (that would represent £1,000 for each of the seven events in heptathlon; a total of £7,000). And do you know what? That's exactly what they did. They gave me a total of £7,000, and they managed to secure me a car for the year, too. The car was heavily branded, but that was all the rage back then. On my little red car in gold writing was, 'Denise going for gold'. Their faith in me felt empowering. They believed in my plan, but more than that: *I* believed in my plan, enough to share it and to sell it to seven strangers.

When someone invests in you financially or emotionally, it becomes more than just material. It gives you the encouragement to keep going with a little more conviction than you had before. Use it and try not to question why. Believe you are deserving and that perhaps there's something more about you than you have given yourself credit for. In time, you will become more adept at accepting help or advice to enhance your progress. It comes full circle in the end, because giving back when and where you can is part of the circle of life and a fundamental part of humanity.

When someone backs you, and you start backing yourself, you have the chance to capitalise on both the sense of responsibility to them that it gives you and the elevation in your self-esteem. It gives you purpose in your workplace, and in relationships. Having someone championing me and seeing my worth throughout my career affected me positively, whether in my ability to train better or as a launchpad into another working environment. I adapted to other people's high expectations of me, believed in myself, and it pushed me to another level of success. You can too: at work; when taking part in a hobby; when you volunteer for a charity or a position to help others in your community. Look for the lifters. And then believe what they say. You are worthy of praise and high expectations.

Write down your plan for success

Journaling as you work on a route to success, professionally or personally, can be a real boost to your self-awareness, thereby keeping you on track. Sometimes we find it easier to plan our home life efficiently, but then we fall apart when getting organised for success at work, or vice versa. Journaling helped with both aspects of my life. You should give it a try. Get yourself a notebook and aim to use it every day, keep it somewhere you can see it, such as next to your bed, on your desk or on the table where you sip your coffee every morning. Make notes on what's going well, how you're feeling, and what you need to improve on. Add any advice you glean from other people. Commit to this practice on paper, as it will help you to shed doubts.

Get started

Here are some prompt questions to get you started with this powerful mindset exercise:

1. Who will be in your support network, both in your personal and professional lives?
2. Can you make a note of the ways each person will support you? This might be monetary support, emotional support or physical support (such as lifts in their car, or offering somewhere to stay), or bringing some fun when you need to let your hair down for a minute and stop taking everything so seriously.

3. Get clear about who will help in what way, and how that will elevate you.

4. Make a note of everything you feel grateful for, today and every day, in all aspects of your life.

5. Finish this sentence: I deserve to be supported at work and at home because...

MAKE CHANGES FOR GREATER SUCCESS

There might come a point when you need to make a change in order to keep moving towards your target. Sometimes, you'll be on the right trajectory and then feel that someone, or something, is slowing you down (for example: a negative friendship circle; a job that steals all your time, confidence and energy with little reward; a bad habit such as vaping or doom scrolling the Internet until the early hours of the morning). For me, the worst time in my life was when I recognised that it was my coach at that time who was slowing me down. I needed someone who could take me to the next level: winning a gold medal. I therefore set my mind to finding a new coach who I believed would get me ready for the 2000 Olympics – not just being up on the podium but standing there holding the gold medal.

I found my dream coach, Charles, who didn't even try to disguise what I needed to do to be successful – but he took some persuading to take me on. Initially he said, 'Well, firstly, you'd have to come to Holland, because I'm not coming to the UK.' And then, he said: 'I just don't know how serious you are about getting to the top.' I replied: 'Pardon me?' We had that sort of dialogue from the get-go: the check and challenge all the time. I wanted to prove him wrong; to prove that he didn't know the core of me and what I was about. He had just seen me as an athlete out there, but he didn't understand the drive that I actually possessed. I literally hounded him until he said: 'OK, let's do a trial. Come out on a training camp with us, and let's see what you've got.' I was ready to show him what I could do. I proved I was worthy of his time, persuading him to work with me using everything I had. Neither of us regretted it.

How to be persuasive

- Don't take no for an answer.
- Find new ways to show off your talents and skills to the person you want to work with.
- Find a back door if the front door is locked.

- Be personable. Part of being persuasive is being *likeable* as a person.
- Don't stop until you get what you want. Perseverance is key.

From then on, it was all about working towards Sydney. We had a few World Championships, European and Commonwealth Games thrown in for good measure, but it was largely about the Sydney Olympics and, unashamedly, upgrading that bronze to a gold. I was one of the best athletes in the world at that point, and I believed in my heart of hearts that I was in a great position to win gold. I had won lots of competitions but getting two silvers at the World Championships had really irked me. It was very frustrating; I had made some little mistakes here and there, while having elevated performances in other areas, but I took that frustration and turned it into fuel.

I remember my coach, Charles, saying to me after those World Championships in 1997: 'You didn't win silver, you lost the gold.' Sabina Braun had been so good in the first two events; she had created a buffer, which I couldn't close. But that comment resonated with me. I was focused on performing better and understanding how to look after my mind. It became almost a central theme for me as a person, as a performer: understanding how much I could actually determine my physical capabilities by matching it with strong mental capacity. I applied it on a daily basis, particularly when injuries set in – of which there were several, including my biggest physical challenge in preparation for Sydney.

Tips for adapting to a sudden slump in mood

Only you have the power to change your vibes, so take control of it. These three things always help me:

1. A good playlist on your device can be the perfect tonic to a slump in mood. Find tracks to make you sing out loud. Go to your favourites from the era when you felt that you had time and energy so that they are packed with good memories.
2. Cold water flannel on the face: you might not fancy it, but you will get a zing from it. It's guaranteed to uplift and energise you instantly.
3. Put on your favourite item of clothing, do your hair or put on some make-up; it might seem silly if you're in your house feeling blue, but it will make

---

you feel good about yourself and put a pep in
your step.

ASK YOURSELF HOW YOU
COPE WITH OBSTACLES

Work on your answers to get better results going forward.
How can you stop yourself from fixating on a mistake or
thinking that you haven't performed as well as you would
like and going into a downward spiral? That's what happened to me before; I was trapped with negative mental
baggage just ahead of the Sydney Olympics in August
2000, because of an injury to my Achilles tendon. This
was the moment that I needed to *adapt*. I couldn't sit in
that feeling of failure, I had to move on. And quickly. How
would *you* do it?

- What obstacles might you face in your career, or
  when finding a balance between work and home,
  or while staying fit when you're so busy?
- How will you keep going when they appear? What
  tools do you have in your toolkit? (Remind yourself
  of this by referring back to page 81.)

- What mindset will you adopt to move through it?
- How important is it to you to keep going and not give in?
- Can you create a mantra – a positive statement, in the present tense – to repeat when things get tough? (For example: *I can do this. I've got what it takes.*)

My Achilles tendon injury resulted in a lot of pain. I couldn't hurdle, I couldn't jump, I couldn't throw, because everything had to be non-weight-bearing to at least take out the inflammation. But instead of feeling defeated, my coach Charles said, 'You've got two arms; you've got your mind. Let's work on that.' And that was the moment in my life where the visualisation piece was so powerful and so important, because I was having to remember what the *physical self* could do, and to get that going on repeat in my brain. I adapted my daily schedule to give me the best chance to get back in the game. I was up early doing physio, then wrapping, which seemed to take forever, to protect my injured Achilles. I even had crutches for a while, but my coach was adamant that we would train around the injury. I would go to the gym, do upper-body work, working out in a way that avoided inflicting any pain or discomfort on the Achilles.

I felt that there was no time to waste with negative emotions, I just had to be doing what I could. I would mentally go through the hurdles, feel myself in the starting blocks, visualise the position I would be in, and what that first foot down would look and feel like if I were able to do it, then I would imagine how I would be running the race. I was going through all this in my mind – and this training was free. I could do it anywhere. I would have my eyes closed, just visualising. I would do my physio and training – in that very light sense of training – then I would go back to my apartment or my room and get into a moment of calm and just play it all through in my head. I used it in the same way that some people use meditation, except that I would do it a bit more often – several times a day – running a particular event or feeling the throw of a javelin using only my mind.

I would also watch sports on TV; immersion consumed my entire world for that period of time when I couldn't physically do much. It kept the negative thoughts at bay, because I knew that I was proactively doing something, I wasn't standing still: I was adapting to the obstacles in my way. I was proactively doing something to combat the negative emotions that could so easily have consumed me, and would have consumed most of us if hit by such a setback. I had every right for it to consume me and to be crying like a baby, but I knew that would be energy that was *not* well spent. I still wanted to be in the black in my energy bank. I still wanted to be in the fight. And you can't do that if you put yourself at a distinct disadvantage mentally. When I look back at that phase of my life, I was rich with knowledge, rich with good habits and application, rich in my ability to adapt to what was in front of me.

That would be my advice to you when hit by an obstacle: think positively, think powerfully, be flexible to any changes in your plan.

PLAN FOR A BIG EVENT

I'm going to tell you how heading off to Australia for the Olympics would change everything for me. This part of the story is about the many elements of planning that enabled me to reach the pinnacle. Of course, I didn't just wake up and find myself there. As you know, I had been planning, preparing, tweaking, checking in with my coach, physio and nutritionist, and making last-minute changes, and I even adopted an alter ego to get me performing at a new level. As I talk you through this story, I would love you to imagine your own journey to the pinnacle, whatever that might mean for you, and think about how much you're prepared to focus, put in the work, do the necessary planning, respond to unexpected obstacles and to *persevere* – perseverance is key.

The closer to the big moment you are, the clearer you

need to be on the minor details of your plan. Whatever you're preparing for (public speaking, a presentation, getting a book deal, or whatever it might be), there will likely be planning involved in the lead-up (such as, research, taking notes, getting help and advice, and so on) as well as planning on the day of the event. Make sure that you're really clear on what you'll need to have in order, on that day, to make sure things will flow as smoothly as possible; for example, what clothes will you be wearing? Do you need to be comfortable, or looking smart? Plan your outfit well ahead of time and make sure it's all ready for the day. How will you wear your hair and make-up (if this is relevant to you), and how much time will you need in order to get ready? Think about the food you'll be eating that will sit comfortably in your body and that you can digest easily. You don't want a rumbling stomach when you're up on stage, but you also don't want to be feeling bloated. Get these details all down on paper, right down to the nitty-gritty details. You'll be doing your future self a favour.

And then to the Olympics. Looking back, it was important for me not to be coddled at that point. I was feeling good, and there was the possibility that I would start to feed off the energies of the people around me – it starts to filter through, almost like osmosis. It kind of gets into you. I think it was a real sense of leadership at that point from my coach Charles, who was very much a team player, but at the point where you need that level of leadership and command, he was more than able to do that in any guise.

From then on, I would think about what I needed to work on; what would make my hurdles really good. Bear in mind that I had not been over any hurdles in the longest period of time, as I had been injured. And here I was, about to hurdle in the most important race of my life. I wasn't thinking about pain, I wasn't smiling, I was just saying to myself: *Of course, I can go over hurdles – I've been doing this for most of my life.*

That tonal shift in the space gave me some inner confidence. After those nine weeks of rehabbing, lying on a physio bed and visualising, working around the skills to keep me busy but not actually doing the hurdle techniques, high-jump run-ups, now it was the day of performance. I had to trust and rely on my wealth of knowledge and experience, setbacks and resilience to come through and execute a performance.

It was an incredible start. I was lined up next to my rival. It was now September; I hadn't run a hurdles race since June. That doesn't usually happen. You'd be losing fitness. That was my race against time really, because I had been fit, but I was missing that last building block, which is peak fitness. I had really felt that I was at a point in my career where I was going to tap into something that I had never tapped into before, on a different level – and then I was struck with that blow. And so I was working and competing on my reserves. I look back and I think: *My goodness, perhaps another week it would be totally different. But gosh, how incredible for you to just demonstrate that fortitude to still compete with the best in the world and still win.*

THE IMPORTANCE OF REST

We all know about the importance of sleep; clocking seven or eight hours a night is the singularly most nourishing thing you can do for yourself. As an athlete, I even learned that a 20-minute power nap in between training sessions or events could be the hit I needed to feel revitalised, mentally and physically, to process the tasks that were to come. We shouldn't underestimate it and should strive to rebalance ourselves when we are stressed or overdoing it. When we don't sleep well, we are more irritable, less tolerant and more likely to make mistakes cognitively or physically. We are looking for optimum performance not only in the sports arena, but also in our chosen professions. We should be aiming for excellence and longevity as people, and something as simple as getting enough rest is in our own hands.

Sometimes, however, like the night before a big event or a job interview, or your child's first day at school, it might be hard to drop off to sleep. You can use a meditation technique such as lying back, closing your eyes and imagining each part of your body relaxing. Here's one that helps me:

- Start with your toes and imagine them sinking into the bed.
- Then your ankles, relaxing down into the bed. Your knees, thighs – and so on, all the way up to your head, by which point you may well already be asleep.
- If you're not, take solace in the knowledge that all rest is good. Just lying down, listening to music or a soothing bedtime story, and letting your limbs relax, is great for you, too. The less pressure you put on yourself to sleep, the more likely you are actually to fall asleep.

FOOD FOR THOUGHT

Learning to fuel myself properly as a heptathlete was crucial to my performance in competitions, and being able to sustain my energy levels effectively during training sessions meant better mental performance, too. At the age of twenty-one, I started making small changes. White sugar to brown, then brown sugar to honey, then honey to no sugar at all. I reduced my fat intake, increased my protein and made sure I was hydrated. These days, I try to make sure I include important things such as vegetables, fruit, oily fish, pulses and beans. When you don't fuel yourself well, you run the risk of fatigue, and you might struggle to concentrate or become irritable. Your gut is your first brain, and treating it with respect will pay dividends. I truly think that you are what you eat, and a balanced diet is one that will support other areas of your life that require mental agility. Forget fads. Good food is your friend.

If you do any endurance events – and yes that includes anything from attending an all-day work conference to taking your kids on a long-haul flight – you need to calculate when your body needs to be replenished before you get to depletion. You're thinking ahead. You're making sure that the grazing, which was my life for so many years – little and often – will keep you going. This can be applied to planning for any event, as sometimes nerves will steal your appetite. Have snacks to hand to nibble on, at all times.

Plan for all eventualities. As an athlete, time would seem to stand still in those early morning hours after breakfast but before an event. You need your body to wake up, but you also need a buffer in case something happens outside your control. You want to make sure that if something does go astray, it's not going to impact the bigger picture, the start time, your preparation, your warm-up time. Over the years, I've learned how long I need to warm up and how to fuel myself efficiently, and I recommend that you do the same, in preparation for any real-time event. Create space around your schedule, plan ahead to pack snacks and enough water. You don't want to be rushing around at the last minute, you want to be focused and grounded and calm, hydrated and fuelled for success.

Stay in your lane

Be aware of your competitors, but don't let them distract you from your performance. Here's how you can stay focused on your success, and not anyone else's:

- Think about what your body needs: food, fuel, exercise, movement.
- Get into the right mindset: positive thoughts only, stay hopeful, optimistic.
- If doubt tries to wriggle its way in, cast it off to space. It has no place here today.
- Do you need to ground yourself? Feel your toes wiggling in your shoes. Feel your weight on the floor.
- Clench and unclench your fists to release stress.

CREATE AN ALTER EGO

You may know that Beyoncé has created an alter ego: Sasha Fierce: someone she becomes before getting on stage. Well, she's not the only one. After a disappointing high jump during the first morning session at the Sydney Olympics, I needed to adjust my mindset to revert to a *winner's mentality.* I had physio, went for lunch, and after that it was to the dorm to rest. I unpacked my bag and repacked it with my shot shoes and sprint spokes. And I remember mentally discarding the shoes that I had worn for the high jump into the corner of my room – putting them away, and knowing I was done with them. I couldn't change the result. I then had a good little sleep, to make up for having been up so early in the morning. I slept well, but I knew that it couldn't be for too long because I didn't want to wake up jaded and lethargic.

On waking again, I had a cold shower and started to get into the mind zone and refocus on the task ahead. I scraped my hair back into a ponytail, as I invariably did for shot-put, and I changed my genre of music: heavy beat and intentional. I wanted it to be aggressive; I needed to pump myself up. I received my call time from my coach, and he said, 'I'm going to come and tap your door, so be ready at 4pm.' My bags were ready to go. I did my drink bottles, my protein, everything was prepared. Just before

4pm, my coach tapped on the door and I literally flung it open, almost like a big reveal, and made an announcement. 'You think you are seeing Denise Lewis here, but you're not. You are seeing Astrid Kumbernuss [who at the time was the world champion shot-putter from Germany] and she's here and present and ready to go!' You've got to think it, you've got to be it: that was my philosophy. My hair was in my power position: I had power hair – whatever you want to call it. Part of that whole masking of self is that you've got to wear the whole ensemble to allow yourself to become that role you are aiming for – your alter ego. And so that's what I did. And I threw well. It was definitely a movement, a mental shift, that had been necessary.

Success on the go

If you're in the middle of a race, presentation, interview or anything that is very time-sensitive, you'll need to have your finger on the pulse at all times. Get yourself in the zone.

- As you transition into the next phase – the next stage of an interview, or returning after a break, for example – look at how it's gone so far. What has worked and what hasn't?

- How can you flex this next stage to really impress everyone?
- What can you pull out of the bag that no one is expecting? Keep some tricks up your sleeve.

HURRY UP AND WAIT

The quote by Phillip C. McGraw, 'Life's a marathon, not a sprint', says it best. We have one life that we are conscious of, and to remain fit for it we have to get in training and set targets. Each new decade of your life will present an opportunity to refresh and examine the previous decade, and it will put down a marker for you to analyse what's worked and what hasn't. The more precise and honest you are with yourself, the more you will be prepared to do the work to improve; the more sophisticated your adaptive skills become, the better you'll be able to handle the challenges that undoubtedly lie ahead.

Reading and soaking in this book gives you a chance to secure the accolade you're seeking. You know what you have to do, as I knew what I had to do to win gold at the

Olympics. Now is the time to believe that you can be successful. What tends to happen when faced with an obstacle in the way of success is that people either fear it or they're not confident. I've seen it happen, when people say, 'You know what, I'm not sure I can run that.' You have to make a decision for yourself about what you're going to do, how you're going to approach your goals, and your life. Get all those little checks crystallised before you start any important move, moment, decision or event.

During training, my coach and I would have worked on discipline, in terms of stamina and staging the various parts of the race. You tend to not go so hard on the first run, because that could have an impact on the rest of your session. But training is different from the actual competition. Then, it's a whole different ball game. You see some people who think: *I'm just going to go*, and you might think: *Gosh, high risk*. But at one point you have to decide with the team what is going to be appropriate for you. Are you going to give it your all for the whole way round (all the laps)? Or are you going to go slower to make it more sustainable throughout? In fact, it's not about sustaining, it's about having *enough left* in the tank to be reactive, trusting that if you run between these margins, it will still be enough. Think about the best strategy for you.

Map out your pinnacle move

Make a note of your answers to the following in your notebook:

1. What would the pinnacle of success be for you?
2. How determined are you to get there?
3. How would it feel to reach the top?
4. How will you celebrate when you get there?
5. What's the next step towards it?

PLAN FOR SUCCESS IN PARENTHOOD

There's a tendency, when we're talking about success, to focus on career success. And that is a huge part of life, but it doesn't have to be all of it. I want to now share an example about how I planned for a different type of success, which was successful motherhood, when I had my fourth child, Troy. By now, I was well versed in motherhood, I had a good understanding of pregnancy, birth and the early days, and so I knew that it would all flow much more smoothly if I put some plans in place. I understood what it meant to take maternity leave – or not – and I knew that if I wanted to have a chance of successfully returning to work *and* bonding with my baby, things needed to change this time. I knew that it would be important to manage people's expectations – and my own – to keep my stress levels in check.

Prioritising your own needs should very much be part of your planning. During pregnancy, I suggested to my husband that he move into the spare room for a few months when the baby arrived, which I know might sound a bit harsh (and I know for some it's simply not a possibility due to not having another bed for the partner to relocate to, even temporarily), but what it meant for us is that I could nurse our baby in the middle of the night without having to worry about waking anyone else. I released my husband from having to do any night feeds and it meant that I remained positive and guilt-free. Instead of being disappointed that he hadn't offered to do a late-evening feed but fell asleep watching football, or that he'd said he would do the 2am feed but remained sleeping, I took ownership from the beginning. I didn't have to nudge him while huffing and puffing every night, which would leave us both awake, with him grumpy and me resentful, as had happened previously. I took control. I had a plan. It felt like a win-win, because in return for my nocturnal sacrifice, he took over as chef for a while – he looked after

me, and I looked after our baby. Simple. Setting your intentions and making them clear will remove unnecessary
disputes once the baby arrives. It's not always so easy to
do this with your first baby, however. Some mothers need
or want help with those early night feeds, and some dads
want to help – but I really recommend it if you have subsequent babies.

Combining work and motherhood takes a lot of
planning, and being adaptable when things don't go as
smoothly as you had envisaged. I had a clear date that I
wanted to return to work: the second week of February,
to be in Birmingham for the 2019 Birmingham Indoor
Athletics Grand Prix. By this point, Troy would be eight
weeks old. Having that target meant that I was focused on
getting to know my baby and his needs, his rhythm, and
working out how to pacify him. I got to know his feeding
pattern, and knew that I could start to express milk and
introduce formula for when I would be on the road. I was
fortunate that the support of my mum, husband and the
newly appointed childcare assistant enabled me to be on the
start line in Birmingham with baby Troy in tow. Making
sure that the wider team – that is, my BBC colleagues, my
editor and production team – were fully aware of what
I needed before making the journey up to Birmingham
that day allowed me to adapt and do something that I
hadn't done before. Working in live telly presents its own

challenges, so to know that I had done all the pre-planning and prep gave me peace of mind to do my other job well. I discovered, while on the job, that it's important to empty your breast milk *before* going on TV, but I only failed to plan for that once!

Going back to work gave me the confidence that at forty-six I was not the geriatric mum the medical profession had labelled me, and that I had the energy and purpose of a thirty-year-old. Women have an immense reservoir of endurance and adaptability, if they believe in themselves. Things are doable when they are given the scope and support to prove it, whatever they want to achieve. I know that going back to work – at all, or after eight weeks' maternity leave – might not be for everyone. You may want or need to spend more time with your family before heading off into your work mind-space again. You may have postnatal depression (PND), or the baby blues, or be recovering from a C-section or other birth complications. The most important thing is that you work to a plan that makes family life successful for you.

Mama's got this

Abbie Ward

Abbie is a key member of the Red Roses, England women's rugby team, and Bristol Bears Women rugby club. Although I have never met Abbie in person, I was struck by her documentary *A Bump in the Road* that explores the challenges of a professional sportswoman and motherhood. I was curious to hear from her how the sporting landscape has changed since I competed being a first-time mum, and what adjustments she made physically and mentally to prepare for motherhood with a view to getting back to the top of her career post pregnancy.

DENISE *A Bump in the Road* was a fascinating watch, showing you and the evolution of not only Rugby Football Union (RFU) sport in general, but also how you strategically planned for your own success and how you adapted. This is so important when you're transitioning from an old job to a new job, and it equally has relevance to going into marriage or new motherhood. Often, when women in sport choose motherhood while they are still competing, they make it look easy, but I know that it isn't. But you have a mindset that allows you to succeed – and you can tell why you've been captain of England, because you're so clear and distinct about how your journey needs to be.

ABBIE Motherhood is hard. People tell you that, but I was actually a bit frustrated about the amount of people during pregnancy who were negative, and saying, 'Oh, just wait for [this to happen]' or 'Wait until [that happens]' and I was thinking: *Why won't someone give me some positivity?* I wanted to share a positive story. Of course, they're all completely correct: it is the hardest thing you'll ever do; it's the hardest thing that *I've* ever done, and I've come back from injuries, ACLs [a ligament injury to the leg], hips, all sorts – and it's something completely different. It's tough going through pregnancy, but actually, for me, the hardest part is now, the time after. When you're a full-time athlete and a full-time mum, you think you've got a day off but then your day off from rugby is a day of full-time mumming, and your day off from mumming is a day of full-time rugby.

DENISE Working mothers need to learn to be flexible.

ABBIE It's really important to be adaptable, but I wouldn't mistake being adaptable for not having a really thorough plan in mind. I plan, but I know within myself that that could change at any time. In those tough days, when things weren't going right, and throughout my career, what I've tried to do is control what can be controlled; for example, I can't control how my body might react to having a baby, but I can influence how it reacts by the rehab I do, by how I eat, how I get rest and how I try to recover. I would look at that rugby pitch in terms of understanding that I can't control the referee's decisions, but I can influence them by my rapport with him and by the pitches that I'm showing him in terms of breakdown. With other things that I am able to influence, I always think about how I can influence them positively. Perhaps it's the athlete in me, but I have the mindset of: *Let's crack on*. People will ask, 'How are you doing this?', 'How are you doing that?', and my reply is always, 'You just do it.'

DENISE From a young age, you've had setbacks, you've had disappointments, you've had other people judging you, you've had an array of negative responses that you've had to overcome – but overcome all of it you did. How can we build our resilience in the face of tough times?

ABBIE I've experienced hardships, setbacks, going without. I tried several different sports and I didn't quite get as far as I wanted to, then I fell into rugby. Being a girl and there not being many contracts, meant that I had to fight for them – it's not easy. I think you learn a lot about mental toughness and resilience through sport. You have to keep building it, because some athletes might get to the top and then lose that edge. In sports, if you take your foot off the pedal, someone will overtake you. I see it now with the girls coming through. They're used to a lot of things being done for them: kit, water bottle, having nutrition, a trainer. It is something I think about a lot as a mum. You want your kids to have everything that they need, but how do you ensure that they work hard, build resilience and have a strong work ethic? I always thought from a young age: *Work hard, play hard* – and that's still what I try to do.

DENISE With my kids, my instinct is to put my foot on the gas and try to make everything easy and right for them, to make sure that they don't fail, whether at school or in those small habits that I think are essential for one's own mental health. I straddle two worlds constantly: being OK to let them fail, to learn about life, while wanting to take care of everything. It's worn me down!

ABBIE I'm sure I will experience that with my children when they get a bit older, but when failing, that's where you can really level up on your adaptability and resilience. Every shirt I get for England genuinely means more than the one before. When talking about playing against Italy, after having my daughter, everyone said, 'Oh Italy – it's not one of their hardest games', but to me that was one of my biggest sporting achievements. It may not be the World Cup final, but because it had been so difficult – having that perspective of not getting chosen, of being dropped, of being injured – it means more. And it's those things that might be considered failures that then allow you to appreciate the wins more: you know the grind that's needed behind the medals. I wish I had had this epiphany years ago. I am now looking at the bigger picture, and it's not just about what I can do for myself. Yes, I want to win more World Cups, but I also want to win grand slams, I want to win premierships, but my focus is on how I can help everyone else and how I can continue to become a better player and a better person. I don't want to fall into these conversations by accident, I want to go after self-improvement actively. I want to see how much growth I can get. I wish I had thought about that when I was twenty as opposed to thirty. I feel that adaptation is about evolution.

DENISE Correct. Even with the pendulum swings of my career, I never lost my core values, and that helped me to navigate any negativity or self-doubt. I don't get really high and I don't get really low, I just stay in my lane, and I don't mind adapting my speed to cruise for a little bit if the answers aren't there.

ABBIE I think you can grow if you're willing to put in the work. It can be done, taking lessons from childhood and onwards, you can keep adapting and improving yourself. When I was twenty-three, I probably thought that I knew it all, that I had all the answers, and as a rugby player I knew exactly what I needed to do. *Pick me, I would think, I can do it all!* Now I think: *What an idiot!* I must have lost my ego to be able to say that I don't have a clue in the grand scheme of things, and there's so much knowledge out there that I still don't have but I want to gain, and I want to have a growth mindset. A lot of the time, people are scared to show their insecurities and vulnerabilities. I was a person who wanted to seem rock solid all the time, dependable and that I knew all the answers. But actually, I think it's *more* powerful to show vulnerabilities, to share them and to say that we've all got them, so it's OK, and we can use them as a strength and a way to connect with those around us. A lot of my new thinking comes from a different perspective and growing up.

DENISE I didn't realise how much impact I was having on others until the last decade, when the mentoring piece of my life has come into play. I can see how integral it is for the young women watching us to have good role models, to get ideas on how to adapt and face change. As you move through your international career into motherhood, growing your leadership qualities, I get a sense that you invite people in rather than pushing them away.

ABBIE If you asked me why I play rugby or what I want to do with rugby, it's to be the best in the world. I love competing. The bigger the game, the better, but I think what I'm now bringing along with that is a bigger picture, and, it's probably because I see that, I know I have to adapt as I get older. Women can be professional rugby players now, which wasn't the case when I started out. I still want to win the World Cup and lift that trophy, but there's a legacy that comes into it now, as I start to think about how many more seasons I have left. I've come to this conclusion at the same time as being a mum, having no spare hours in the day, but if I can try to do it all, I will.

DENISE I'm going to take you back just a little bit. You would have faced all those questions: 'Why is she doing rugby?', 'That's not very feminine.' How did you adapt your self-belief in the face of other people's negativity?

ABBIE Firstly, for all of us, a lot of it should be to just ignore it, make it white noise. I guess I'm headstrong, I always have been. So, if someone says to me, 'You can't do that', my reaction is, 'Watch me.' I've had really strong values, so for example, I found it really hard to take when there weren't contracts for the women in rugby, but there have always been contracts for the men. When I went to university, there was one point where I had had a conversation with my dad and he said, 'Perhaps you need to stop playing rugby and concentrate on school.' And I knew that if I was his son, we wouldn't be having that conversation. I think that unfairness made me dig even deeper to smash the glass ceiling. Secondly, it's about surrounding yourself with the right people. Around rugby people, no one is asking, 'Why are you doing that?', 'Why do you look like that?' Find your support network.

DENISE I speak to some women, and many women of colour, who feel held back because they are the first. But sometimes it's about flipping that switch and the narrative and saying, 'I am the first, and I'm going to own my space instead of cowering.'

ABBIE We should all try to be that pioneer, that person who paves the way, if there is something we feel passionate about. It might get really uncomfortable, really hard, but if it hasn't been done by anyone else yet, just go and do it – ignore the doubters and cynics. They can adapt to you, so make space for yourself.

––––

YOU CAN'T PLAN FOR EVERYTHING

I've shared with you the meticulous planning I did when preparing for career success, and competing at the Olympics, as well as when preparing for fourth-time motherhood, but the truth is that you're never going to be able to completely control everything. You might go for a stable job so that you can get the mortgage, only to be told that you need to reinterview for your job one day. Life keeps us on our toes – and you're going to need to be ready to adapt your plan, at any given moment.

Keep checking in with yourself: what are your new markers? What would you like to accomplish? Has the target moved? Are you nimble and willing to move with those targets? Monitor your progress, look at what's going well and what needs tweaking, and remember that it's OK to need to make changes. This is all part of 'success' – it's rarely linear. When unforeseeable events occur, be ready for them, as best you can. Think ahead and plan for all sorts of curveballs so that when one drops in, you're ready to flex around it, finding versatility in yourself as you head to victory.

Five ways to plan for success

1. Get clear on what it is you would like to achieve. Write it down. Read it back.
2. Identify what it is that you will need to sacrifice in order to achieve it.
3. Decide who you need in your support network.
4. Prepare for inevitable obstacles along the way.
5. Bask in the glow of success when you get there. Well done you, it's never, ever easy.

CHAPTER 4

Follow Your Instincts

Follow your instincts. That's where true
wisdom manifests itself.

OPRAH WINFREY

As soon as a baby is born, they are led by instinct. Their
body tells them that it's time to feed, sleep and be close to
their mother. Instinct, you see, is the more physical reaction, whereas intellect is about the mind. We grow into
children, then adults, and we still pay attention to what
cues our body is giving us: hunger, tiredness, needing
movement, sorrow, desiring physical touch or comfort,
and so on. It often gets diluted when we are inevitably
distracted by external forces, but we need to refocus on

it. Trusting your gut feeling could seem counterintuitive to adaptability, but when it leads to better self-awareness, I think they can go hand in hand. A gut feeling is the protector – the caution provider – that should lead you to ask further questions of a situation, and the answers could lead you to a positive change. Unlocking your gut instinct can help you listen to your heart and your head, and not second-guess yourself when you're adapting to something that feels new or scary.

Perhaps you know what you want to do with your life, and you feel it so deeply in your soul that every time you dream of that different type of life you feel warm and glowing. Perhaps you've had that gut reaction to someone you're supposed to be working with, but for whatever reason, it just doesn't feel right in your stomach. Or perhaps, as a mother, you've had to follow your instincts in deciding what it is that your child needs in order to be safe, well and happy.

This chapter is about using your instinct to make big and small life decisions and how you can be ready to swap and move quickly when you can sense something no longer feels right. I'll share examples of when I've followed my gut and it's gone to plan. How many times have you said to yourself: *I should have followed my instincts*, or *I knew something wasn't right about this situation*? Following your instincts can help you to navigate uncertain situations, or once you've weighed up a host of options about what to do, you can *then* follow your gut feeling. It can be very useful when assessing new information, and planning a route forward.

USE INSTINCT TO FIND YOUR RIGHT PATH

Some of us are lucky enough to find a path we want to be on at a fairly young age, which we can then pursue into adulthood. But others among us might not manage to work out what we would enjoy or what we would like to be doing, or we might be led away from a passion because a parent, carer or teacher thinks that we should be focusing elsewhere. By reflecting on these formative years, we can start to understand how we've got to where we are today. Also, remember that it's never too late to try something new that feels right for your soul, and so, if you were forced to leave behind something that you truly loved doing, perhaps you can return to it now, in your present life.

Notes on how you became you

Make a note of your answers to the following:

1. Think back to your time at school. What did you feel passionate about? Often, reflecting on the first seven years of our life can help us to see where our deep passions lie.
2. In what ways has this fed into the life you lead now?
3. If you left behind a passion and moved in a different direction, would you like to re-engage with it now?
4. Were you encouraged to stay on a path you liked, or were you led elsewhere?
5. Make some notes on what you were like, as a school-aged child, and what you're like now. In what ways are you similar, and in what ways have you changed?
6. How would you like to bring that hopeful kid back into the you of today?

WHAT CAN HAPPEN WHEN YOU IGNORE YOUR INSTINCT?

There is no greater feeling than trusting your instincts: making a decision based on a visceral feeling and seeing that you've got it right. It feels so good in your body and mind, knowing that you can trust yourself. But sometimes we ignore the physical message our body is sending us because the mind is suggesting that there might be something else we would prefer to be doing. Our judgement can become clouded. And this can have disastrous consequences, as I was to discover for myself after ignoring a clear message that a change needed to be made and realising later that my lack of adaptability in that moment was partly what ended my athletics career.

After winning gold at the Olympics – and all the subsequent celebrations and engagements that came with my victory – I needed a break from it all, so I went to Jamaica. I wanted to show my uncle Jack my medal. He was so proud, and the local newspaper did a feature on me, which was lovely. But my Dutch doctor hadn't wanted me to go, as he said I needed surgery and it would have required me to be laid up for months, if I went ahead. He warned me clearly, 'This is the window; you need to do it, otherwise it's going to be impossible.' It niggled inside me that he was right, but I decided not to take his advice. I told myself that I needed a holiday – it's what I always did at the end of the season. I had to live with the consequences of my stubbornness, however, which really cost me later on. All I had ever known in terms of work and focus was quickly shifting, and perhaps I wasn't good at listening to my instincts and being adaptable back then. I urge you to listen to your body alongside your gut, if anything is ever physically niggling at you, and to listen to advice from the experts around you, because ignoring these red flags can have dire consequences further down the line.

 Reflect on your instincts

Make a note of your answers to the following:

1. Have you ever gone against your instinct?
2. What was the consequence?
3. When have you followed your instinct and seen it work out well?
4. How did that feel?
5. Is there anything you have a strong feeling about now that you need to act on?

LISTEN TO YOUR HEART

Sometimes we make life plans. At other times, life throws something at us and we have to decide whether we're going to roll with it or move in a different direction. There are consequences to whatever decision we make, so this is a real test of whether you can listen to your heart's calling or if you're distracted by the ego or the opinions being thrown at you. If you have a big decision to make and you can't decide what you want to do, take a moment to sit alone in a peaceful environment and close your eyes. Put your hand on your heart and remind yourself that you have all the answers you need, within yourself. Often, you know what you want and need to do, but other people are distracting you from this truth, or they are making it too noisy for you to hear it. Shush that drama. When you are alone, ask yourself: *What do I need, right now?* Sit in the silence, don't force anything, and see what lands for you. It might be a sudden answer: *Leave* or *stay put.* Or it might be a vision of something from the past that then triggers a new line of thinking. Basically, we're trying to quieten all the other voices so that you can hear your own. Because, really, it's your decision alone, and it is you, first and foremost, who will have to live with the outcome.

An example of this is when I pulled out after the fifth

event, the long jump, at the 2004 Olympics, and asked the Team GB organisers to get me on the next flight out of there ASAP because I couldn't deal with being in that environment any longer. I remember flying back from Athens disappointed but knowing that I had followed my instinct, which was screaming at me to *get the hell out of there and get back home!* And what happened when I got home? There was a surprising little detour on my career path that my gut told me to go for. I was asked to go on *Strictly Come Dancing*, which reawakened something in me. It was a tonic when I needed one, as my gut had reassured me it would be.

To the rest of the world – and possibly to myself – I felt like a failure, because we were all expecting me to be on a podium. It was a horrid time. And that's why having something fun and bright to look forward to, *Strictly*, where there wasn't such an emotional investment, helped me. I didn't have time to think about the disappointment of athletics, but I still had a different type of competition and performance that warmed my heart when it needed it most. I adapted my short-term goals to get me through a hard time in my life.

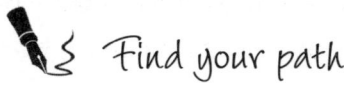 *Find your path*

Make a note of your answers to the following:

1. Have you ever been diverted from your path?
2. What positives do you attach to the new path?
3. What challenges did that shift bring with it?
4. If you could go back, would you make the same decision again?
5. What did that big life change teach you, moving forward?

At that stage, I still hadn't told myself that I was retired from athletics, even though I knew my career wasn't the same, and my coach Charles told me that he was going back to the Netherlands, so I would be coachless again. That was pending in the new year of 2005. I would be back at career square one. And my private life wasn't easy at that time either. My grandmother was diagnosed with breast cancer while I was doing *Strictly*, so I was trying to be brave while my heart was breaking, as we'd always been very close. On 5 February she died. By then, I had moved back to the Midlands, so I was able to spend time with her, and then, when she was hospital-bound, I could do all the shuttle runs for family members who were flying in from overseas. There was nothing left for me to do when we lost her, my heart had gone out of everything.

That was the point at which I realised I had to stop athletics. I had lost my mojo, and I didn't have the strength to start looking for another coach, so I announced that I was going to retire, and I just kind of tiptoed out of sport. It was a very strange moment, driven by quiet instinct, led by my broken heart. There was no fanfare, as such. I remember doing an interview with a features writer for *The Times* but, other than that, it was just an ending. Full stop. It might be my bad memory but I don't recall a 'thank you', or a 'thanks for your years of service'. But it could be the haze. I didn't want it, anyway. It was strange to not have the ending marked in some way, though. I was just gone.

Go your own way

Tanja Spittal

Here I include a conversation with Tanja Spittal, a specialist career coach, on going with your gut and choosing something different for yourself.

Tanja and I met on the school run back in 2009 when

my oldest son was three. Our sons became friends and have stayed friends since – and so have we. She was one of the mums who always looked totally in control of themselves, even in the school environment, which can often be a scary place for mums who are trying to work out the school politics and cliques. She was one of the more mature parents (she had two older children), and I warmed to her energy and positivity instantly. With these attributes, it was obvious to me why she was the class representative and chaired the school parents' association, tasked with fundraising activities and being a voice for parents in meetings with the headteacher or school governors. But the more I got to know Tanja, the more it became evident that she was not living the charmed life that everyone perceived. On one hand, she was living in a big house in a leafy suburb and didn't want for anything, with a hard-working husband supporting her, but on the other hand, her self-worth was at an all-time low. Somehow, however, she found the courage to step out of her comfort zone and challenge herself, escaping the niggling resentment she felt at being ignored since becoming a mother.

DENISE Do you think an ability to adapt comes naturally to most of us, or does it take a growth mindset to seek change and self-improvement in life in the way that you did?

TANJA I think being older helps. I'm different now from how I was. When I was in my late thirties/forties, when the children were six upwards, I was trying to find what I wanted to do. I had been a lawyer before children and I sat on the appeals panel at Bucks County Council, which gave me the confidence that I could take on the school roles you mentioned. The confidence came from being able to sit on a panel with other men, predominantly, and say, 'I'm the legal entity' or 'the non-legal entity'. Immediately you get a bit more respect. When the children were older, I started thinking: *What else can I do?* They don't need me as much, so I need to think about what my skill set is. I had a legal background, but I didn't want to go back into the law. I'm sociable, and I had also worked as a legal recruiter, but I didn't want to go back into recruitment because you'd have to headhunt or executive-search from home. Then I thought: *Aha! What about being an estate agent? Selling houses is the same as selling people into jobs.* I reached out to three people I knew in the estate-agent industry, and a local mum was setting up an estate agency. She sweetly invited me to do a joint venture with a guy they had asked to set up and open in a new location. He hired me as the office manager and he made a point of appreciating that I was good with people; I got a little bit more confident working on the computer, and putting brochures and marketing materials together. After a year of doing that, I met up with Reignite Academy, connecting through Giraffe Coaching – a small local business that I co-founded to help women find a focus after a career break – and was asked to work for them. I could use my coaching skills and legal background, to streamline people's re-entry into the workforce.

DENISE From being legally trained to a stay-at-home mum for ten years, to getting into business, how was that to navigate?

TANJA I wasn't good at being a lawyer; it just doesn't suit me. I lasted two years doing that, and then moved into legal recruitment, which I was good at. But I chose to be a full-time mum because my husband, Phillip, was earning good money and he was never at home, trying to rise to partner at his legal firm. I had two children, seventeen months apart, and then five years later our youngest came along. I soon realised, though, that being a mum and helping at the school wasn't enough for me. I needed to be more intellectually challenged. I remember someone coaching me, and they said, 'What do you want?', and I said, 'I want to be a go-to person for someone', and that's when I set up my career-coaching business during the pandemic. It was originally because of boredom and the lack of intellectual stimulation; I could be doing something which made me feel good – and which impressed other people. I needed my husband and my mum to say, 'Oh wow! That's really good', which I had never had.

DENISE You wanted to impress your husband and let him see you were more capable than just a mum being at home, but your mum was also a huge influence on how you viewed yourself. You wanted to impress her. You're an only child, like me. Was that relationship with her intense?

TANJA Completely. A healer once did these stones on me, and she identified my mantra, or my thing, as a fear of disappointing others – and I always remember that. But I feel very secure in what I have here in the home, and my mum always taught me that you can overcome anything – well, most problems. I'm inwardly confident. And with age and experience, we can be more assertive and get over the imposter syndrome of our youth. A lot of candidates I speak to who are going back into law, and who are uber-bright and have got a wealth of experience, often say to me, 'Oh, I don't think I can do it.' But they can. They have done it before. There is a thing called an 'insecure overachiever': they're always insecure, because they've got such high standards. My approach is to make it good enough, *not* that it has to be perfect.

DENISE Do you think you could have prevented certain experiences in your twenties and thirties if you had had a different mindset?

TANJA You can't change the past, but I'm content looking back. I probably wouldn't have qualified as a lawyer if I had really thought about who I was and my skill sets – I followed what my mother told me, pretty much, and did it. I don't regret that. I've had a non-linear career, but now it's come full circle and I'm content. A legal qualification, recruitment skill set, coaching, being with people and making them feel good. We all have different mindsets, and different senses of self-fulfilment. I have to remind myself that some people might be happy *not* having jobs. I have had the luxury of money and being able to decide on a whim what I want to do, and then going for it.

DENISE Even with money, you weren't happy at one point in your life, but you got up and did something about it. That's not easy.

TANJA I was trying to find out what would satisfy me, and money enabled me to do that because I didn't have to earn a living. I don't think everyone has that need or thirst for something outside the home, but financial independence is really important to me. I don't know if it comes from the law or from my mother, but it's a massive thing.

DENISE You had a mum who was a single parent and struggled financially. I come from a line of Caribbean immigrants arriving in this country needing to prove themselves, and I'm an extension of that. But as we've moved through the generations where women want more choice, I think it's actually becoming harder because there's the expectation that you can have it all: be the working mum; earn a living; have children; fit in the Pilates; look great; and be amazing – but at what cost?

TANJA About women's multiple identities, can I just say one point: with age, you become more honest about yourself and showing your true self. You don't have your public persona and your personal persona, do you? When you look back and think about your identity in your twenties, do you think that was the real you? I think that I'm almost 90 per cent me most of the time now, which is lovely. I was probably only 35 per cent or 40 per cent me in all those other roles, and in my twenties.

DENISE This is the beauty of ageing. Some people hate it, some people will say, 'How can you say that?' Because when you get older, everything starts to hurt, but you get to own your space more, the older you get.

TANJA I tell everybody I'm a middle-aged, menopausal mother and I love it because I'm assertive and I am me – more than I ever was before.

———

HOW INSTINCT HAS GUIDED MY CAREER DECISIONS

Now, let's get into the nitty-gritty of how I used my instinct specifically in sports. There was of course that decision, quite early on – in 1996 – about moving from one coach to another. That was very much led by instinct. It came from within. There was an element of intellect involved, but it was largely my body telling me what to do. My body will often feel uncomfortable about a situation and then I'll ask myself: *Why are you feeling like that? What is that about?* And then there's this bounce between body and mind.

My sense was that I could no longer trust what my first coach was saying to me. I wasn't happy there, I wasn't feeling that the environment was good for me any more, so my brain kicked into gear and asked what I was going to do about it. And that's where the planning starts. *What are you going to do? Where are you going to go? Who are you going to work with? Are you prepared to leave this place that is your home? If yes, then what next?* But all too often you think: *Well, that's going to be too difficult. No, I'm not going to do it. No, it's better to stay. I'm sure this will pass.* This is what we know about how the mind works, so you have to then listen to the clear signals given to you by your body.

I had this heightened sense that was making me act. I didn't really know where to go, but I just knew this direction wasn't right. It couldn't bear any more fruit, so I needed to adapt – and adapt quickly. I guess in other life situations, you do have to think a bit more carefully, because you might need to consider the impact of a snap decision: *If I leave this job, will I find another one? Am I prepared to take a pay cut for my happiness? What's the journey time?* And all the other life factors that you have to think about when you are weighing up what to do. But I went for it. I did it, because there was an absolute sense of: *I've got to make these changes.* Once I had made the change, and I could see that I had been right, I was able to trust myself even more. It gave me confidence, knowing that my instinct had been right. Have you also felt empowered when you've followed your gut?

Of course, there have also been times when I've felt lost, so I haven't backed myself, and then I've gone along with something that wasn't right. It's during those periods that I've hit stumbling blocks and ended up in a bit of a spiral. Conversely, when I've found it in myself to make a decision and to make a change, to back myself and make sure that I'm committed in my mind, that's when exciting change happens. If I went with the new coach, Charles, I was going to have to move to Holland – a big adaptation to my daily life. But the ability to adapt to that new environment was critical. It was a different language, a totally different environment and a totally different coaching approach. But it helped to know that it was going to be sticky at first, and a bit uncomfortable, but I felt prepared for that – plus I remembered why I had made the change and what I hoped to get out of it.

Following your instincts won't always be the easiest path, or the smoothest. You've got to listen to the calling, make the change, work through it and accept that you won't know the outcome for sure until you get there. You have to stick with your gut and keep going a bit longer. You can't quit while following a new path that you feel is going to be right in the long run – be it an athletics coach, or a job, or a relationship. You have to give it a chance, and before you know it, whatever the change is that you've made, whatever chance you've taken, if your gut is still telling you that it was the right thing to do, it will eventually start to feel like your new norm – a *better* norm.

 think about your career decisions

Make a note of your answers to the following:

1. What career decisions have you made that were guided by instinct?
2. How have they worked out?
3. Are there any decisions you made that other people couldn't understand?
4. Are you in a situation right now that needs an answer?
5. Can you hear what your body is saying about it?

SAY YES TO SAYING NO

There have been times when I've recognised that I'm doing too much. I used to overload my diary, going from event to event because I thought I had to be seen. I wanted to represent communities that were important to me, and I was more concerned how it would be perceived if I said no to something I was asked to attend. What people don't always realise is that events clash and, with a young family, having back-to-back events will impact your energy, let alone all the added work of sorting outfits and the preparation of getting ready.

You have to say no sometimes. Not saying so is what leads women into burnout: the feeling that you've got to keep going and giving, losing yourself, and often your good health and happiness, in the process. What do you feel and need? That's something that no one else can answer for you at that moment. And so, for example, when you turn down an invite, think about what it might cost you by not going. Perhaps you won't get an invite next year, but do you care? You have to realise that you'll be all right, there will always be something else, and then you have to remind yourself of all the really good things that you do already, and that perhaps you deserve a break. I've learned: if in doubt, just say no.

INSTINCT IN CHILDBIRTH

What greater instinct is there than when a woman gives birth? In fact, the whole journey of motherhood is just packed with instinct: listening to your body, working out what it needs, slowing down when that's the message you're getting. I actually loved pregnancy. In the first few weeks, I had a feeling of nausea and I had to keep grazing – not unlike when I was competing as an athlete, little and often – but other than that first trimester nausea, I was fine. I'm very fortunate that my body has adapted well to all my pregnancies, so physically and mentally I gave over to it.

The first time round, when I was pregnant with Lauryn, I could really feel each change in my body. There was a little bit of discomfort – obviously I had very tight, strong abs, so those first separations of the abs were difficult – but otherwise, that pregnancy was OK. The birth was hard, though. I was almost wired to the bed. I ended up having an epidural which worked on only half my body and Lauryn ended up having a ventouse to pull her out: a vacuum extraction which meant that her head was a cone shape for days. That experience with Lauryn definitely shaped my instincts about what I wanted with the next two births. Ryan and Kane were born in the water, using the breathing techniques that I had learned. It felt right, magical. I had my own music playing, and I was really feeling what was happening to me. I had practised pregnancy yoga in the lead-up, which was just fantastic, and when Kane shot into the water it was like a missile. I had been saying, 'Where's the baby? Where did he go?' But they had it covered.

Sadly, I was too old to have a water birth with Troy, my fourth. I was forty-six and they referred to me as a geriatric mum – a lovely term, used for any mother over the age of thirty-nine. I was not happy about any of it. I asked to speak to the head matron, because a consultant at one of the hospitals said that I wouldn't be allowed on a midwife-led ward because I was too high risk. It felt like there were lots of roadblocks from the get-go, and so it took me a long while to decide where I wanted to have Troy. Luckily, I had good midwives on the day. My waters had broken, but then I had no contractions, so I had to go in to make sure that there wasn't an infection. I knew that if they started with interventions, it would be interventions all the way, so I was trying to keep calm, trust my motherly instincts, and keep my body and mind engaged. I really didn't want to go down the C-section route, but there came a point when I thought: *If the baby is in jeopardy, obviously that's what we'll do.*

The baby's heart rate was dropping too low and we were playing this dicey game, which felt risky. There was a point at which Troy's heart rate was so low that they brought in a couple of consultants. That was the only time I got emotional. I was thinking: *We've got this far, the both of us, I just can't imagine not being able to do this.* And I remember saying to Steve that if it had to be a C-section, let's just do it. Let's make that decision now and get the baby out safely. I had a little weep and the consultant came in, then suddenly, there was very strong leadership. 'No, you're going to do this,' he said. 'You'll be fine, and baby's fine. You'll be all right.' And so we got to work. It felt momentous. Little Troy came out. The gift of life. It's unbelievable. It is remarkable. Those little humans, little beans.

Steve actually videoed this one, knowing that it was going to be the last. I've watched it a couple of times, just to remind myself how, at forty-six, when they thought it wasn't possible, that it was high risk, we did it. I'm not necessarily saying that I would advise having a baby in your late forties, but I know that there are so many more women having their first child later, because of the choices they have made about their careers, or because they hadn't found the right partner; they mustn't be discouraged by the narrative out there about: 'thirty years from now, where are you going to be?' People judge your choices, but the future self is something none of us are guaranteed, so why not choose to be present right now? Have the baby, or don't have the baby; become a mum when it feels right for you, not anyone else – because you will end up doing the lion's share of the work and the worrying. Follow your instincts, mama.

How did your gut instinct kick in during childbirth?

- If you're a mother, how were you led by instinct during childbirth? This most primal experience is worth reflecting on, deeply, to remind yourself of one of the most important times in your life when you've relied on listening to your body and trusting that it knows what it needs to do.

- How did it feel, to be fully present in that moment? Being able to access that same focus and determination in other situations is invaluable. Letting everything else drop away and keeping the focus on the one – incredibly important – thing that you're trying to achieve.

- Did you feel well supported, at that time? Even when we're razor-focused and clear on what we need to do, we can rely on others to support us. It's integral to almost every process, having that support.

- Which one word would you use to describe that moment of new motherhood? I wonder if you felt as you expected you would, or differently?

PARENTING FROM THE GUT

In most cases, instinct as a parent is naturally very strong, and it kicks in the minute a child is born. The sense that: *This is what my child needs at this moment*, or *This is what I should be doing for them right now*, is second nature. The only thing that takes me off-course is sometimes not being on the same page as my husband, which makes me question myself. I have to work out whether it should be a case of 'my way or the highway', or is it really that I'm just missing the mark and he's right? After all, he is the only other person on the planet who knows and loves our children as much as I do.

We mums are wired differently, however, aren't we – for good or bad? I've heard that when you're nurturing children all the time, there's a lobe in your brain that is increased. That intense caring gives you a 'sense' about what is now needed. It's like the third eye that is spoken about in Hinduism (representing wisdom and enlightenment), and it's omnipresent. It's just there. I certainly have that sixth sense, and I'm sure that most other mothers do, too; for example, I have this intuition sometimes, when one of my children comes home with a look on their face that I just know there's something up. At first, they might say that they're fine or resist giving me any information, but I can sense it. I run through the possibilities: what were they doing? What might they have found hard? Is this about someone else? And often I will have the realisation about what it might be before they even tell me. I've adapted my problem-solving skills to use non-verbal communication with them when they are like this. My love for them is like nothing I've known. I would adapt anything in my life if they were feeling terrible, and me making a change could make them happy or healthy.

With our careers, we might have big ambitions and work hard towards them, but ultimately, if it doesn't happen, it's not a life-or-death situation. It's just disappointing. With a child, though, especially when they're babies, you're listening to their cry and working out what they need to actually keep them alive: it *is* a matter of life or death.

 How do you use your instincts as a parent?

Make a note of your answers to the following:

1. Can you think of three examples when you've followed your instinct in parenting?
2. What was the outcome?
3. What barriers do you face in motherhood when it comes to following your instinct?

> 4. How does your family react when you 'just know'?
>
> 5. Are there any times you wish you had done things differently?

When it comes to other people looking after our children – at school or nursery – our gut instincts need to go up another level. I remember with one of my sons, his school was trying to label him as being trouble when I knew that wasn't really him. He was too young to be given that label and they needed to look deeper into the situation, but they weren't prepared to do that, so I moved him to a new school. That's what my gut was telling me to do, as they weren't doing anything for his confidence, having pigeon-holed him in that way. He didn't deserve that. I could see that he was feeling frustrated, and there were some issues that possibly needed further examination, but that needed to be done with compassion. When he joined the new school, I was given reassurance and signposted towards the additional support he might need; for example, I could see that he hated reading, which meant that in a classroom setting he was frustrated because he couldn't follow what was going on. He wasn't naughty; he was struggling. It takes a teacher who is willing to be kind, compassionate and patient to see what a child's needs are and how they can be met. Thankfully, he got that at the new school. Thank God for my gut.

Motherhood is the hardest job that I've ever had. Especially mothering teenagers, as I said in the previous chapter. You have to trust your gut, while allowing them to hone their own, working some things out for them while letting them work out other things for themselves. I try to catch them on their own and when they're not distracted by devices: usually car journeys are a good time for a chat. I'll hear them out, but sometimes I have to make strong suggestions. With one of them, I could see that he receives information better from his dad, so I make suggestions to Steve about what I feel instinctively, and I ask him to do the delivery.

I know that I'm usually the one telling the kids what to do, and sometimes they get fed up with hearing it from me. For boys who are becoming men, that can be triggering. I know when to take a step back and see that I can't be everyone and everything to them, it's about letting go. It's painful for me, because I want to fix everything, but there are times when the information coming from a different source will be much more powerful. Also, it's a way to preserve a relationship. It doesn't lessen me, or make me seem like a weaker person – on the contrary: there's great strength in the realisation that it's not about me, it's about them and what each of them need, individually, and how they will best receive that. I hope you remember that, too, in your trying times with children, especially teenagers. To still love them, to listen to them and to allow them to forge ahead without you, takes a really brilliant mum.

It could be likened to an office environment and having a workforce. You've got the senior leadership teams working out who within that team are able to deliver information in a way that people will understand and that will reduce the potential conflict, thereby getting you to the end result sooner. It's a people skill, I think. And it requires you to let go of the ego, because, as mothers, we might think that we should be able to do everything, but sometimes, like in a work environment, it's about delegating.

FEEL YOUR SPIRITUAL SIDE

Church has played a big part in my life. I feel comforted by the sense that there is something else out there, as well as having a connection to the land and cosmos. It's not really deep, just a pleasant feeling about what else might be there. When my great-grandmother was alive and I used to go back to Jamaica, we would always go to church. It was a big thing for her. And church in Jamaica is intense. Not only is it bloody hot and they've got these little fans blowing heat around the church, but it's also quite long. I've always been appreciative of the sense of direction it gives people, though, and the purpose. I used to say my prayers daily, and I can always tell when my mum's been with my son, Troy, a little bit longer than just a couple of days, because then he's saying his prayers too. It was one of the things I always tried to encourage my children to do: say prayers when they were little, just giving thanks. Whether it's religion or gratitude, I don't know.

When I feel emotionally fragile or at a low point, I find space and the strength to believe things will get better by listening to a song by Faith Evan called 'Keep the Faith'. My mum raised me to believe that spirituality, religion or connection comes from within. We shouldn't feel forced to go to an institution to believe in a higher power, to show gratitude or to pray. I agree with her. Spirituality is a very personal journey. Understanding that there's more out there than we understand, trying to see the good in others, and being a good person, gives everyone a positive spirituality that radiates out of them, without ever stepping into a religious building.

I believe that there is a higher force that I lean into in tough times; a belief that keeps me morally accountable and guides my values. It doesn't mean that I don't make mistakes, but it does give me an opportunity to have a conscious dialogue with myself to make amends, to forgive myself and to adapt my choices to do better next time. Spirituality helps to build courage in changing times and to give us a positive outlook during troubling moments. To me, spirituality allows us to see the world with fresh eyes and to feel it with a brave heart. My faith in the universe – and in myself – has allowed me to push through turmoil and move on, knowing that things will get better, trusting the connections I have in my life, feeling inherently grateful for everything I have.

You can call it spirituality or simply a sense of connection to something bigger than yourself, whether it's the natural world or a higher being; it is an external power that some of us feel in the same way as a sense of an internal power that we all need to tap into. My main goal in writing this book was to empower you to believe in yourself, and to remind you that your self-empowerment will grow when you nurture the skills of adaptability. The more you can embrace new circumstances, adjust to challenges or learn from life's twists and turns, the more you will grow in every aspect of your life.

Being fearful of the unknown will keep you stuck. Allowing yourself to bathe in positivity rather than negativity is a choice, however. I hope that this book will boost your ability to be your own hype person and life coach, giving you the skills that you need to flip to a narrative that serves you best, whatever life throws at you. The ability to trust your instincts through tough times lies in the way that you choose to seek inner peace, reflect on change and reconnect with your deepest self. Acts of self-kindness will help you focus on your purpose and passions without getting weighed down by other people's expectations. Spirituality and adaptability work together to keep you on track, powering up your agility and ability to be resilient – and they radiate everything that is powerfully, beautifully and uniquely you.

Believe me, I know. During some of the hardest situations in my life, I have definitely given over to a greater energy. Especially when I haven't been able to see the way through immediately. I've asked: 'What do I need to do, at this moment?' And I've handed over a certain amount of responsibility. I'm not sure if it's to a God of sorts or to my higher consciousness, to my inner gut. Once the message drops, and I'm back in action, I often think: *OK, there's got to be a lesson here. What should I be feeling? Should I just be patient? Should I find calm?* I feel comforted by the sense that there is an energy out there, around me and within me.

While going into labour with each of my babies, I was asking for strength to guide my baby out of my body and into the world. That miracle of life. I never prayed for a gold medal, though. I never prayed for the outcome of my sporting competitions. I would just ask for strength of character, strength of understanding, to be able to apply myself to the task, especially when it was getting difficult. I would ask for support in what might be a changeable, unpredictable event. I would also include in prayer those times when I knew that I might not get what I wanted and would need to pick myself up again: to be able to keep going, despite disappointment.

In my life, I've had a lot of really good things happen, but I've also been through some really hard periods. I've experienced both ends of the spectrum. I look at how I've managed to allow the two different emotions to coexist within me, and I wonder if that's from leaning on a bigger energy, outside myself. I've managed to find the strength to centre on the successes and learn from the difficulties when I've needed to adapt to such things, and I'm grateful for that ability.

INTUITIVELY YOU

You have to learn to listen to your instinct, without reacting too quickly, too emotionally, even if you have a strong sense that something is right or wrong. Sometimes you need a bit of space after an event before reacting. I'm trying to get better at this, but I'm still a work in progress. Rather than having an emotional outburst, I try to leave some time before responding. Having a dialogue with other people is important, too, to help you order your thoughts. They might give you a new perspective that helps you to see that you've missed something. As individuals, we seek comfort in others, and reassurances. Over the last five years, I've started to open up more. I remember once having a woman chauffeur I could talk to deeply. We found a real connection. I was raised to be very private – my mum's private, my grandmother was also very private – but I've found this ability to share my thoughts and have open conversations, which is quite therapeutic at times and gives me a better understanding of others.

I have my instant response, and then I pause. If I can talk to a trusted friend, I do. And then I sit down and think: *OK, how do I feel now?* I think it's quite simple, really. Quite basic. You listen, talk it out, ask questions, write some notes, sit with your thoughts, re-examine your feelings and ultimately make a decision about what needs to happen next.

Work on honing your instincts

Make a note of your answers to the following:

1. What do you do when you're not sure about the decision you would like to make?
2. Who do you lean on, in those times?
3. Which rituals or activities connect you with your instinct?
4. What do you do if you feel overwhelmed or have spiralling thoughts?
5. How can you connect more deeply with your instinct, going forwards?

In the evenings, I listen to the Calm app and meditate for ten minutes. You can do meditation without an app, as long as you really do focus on the positive conversation that you need to have with yourself. That's my form of visualisation. I set myself up to think and feel positive thoughts – and I give over to that. I try to remember that things are transient and that this intense state of emotion is not permanent. I am not defined by it. Sometimes, I need to lie down if I'm really upset and to sleep off the sorrow. I find that very comforting.

Another tool I use is journaling, as you can probably tell from the amount of journal prompt questions I've littered across the pages of this book where you see the pen illustration. I encourage you to take up this habit that has helped me so much. I said earlier that I used to keep a diary in the early stages of athletics to note down how I was feeling, what had happened, how the training sessions went and how I felt post-training. The training diary was a good tool for getting the emotion out, and I would always add a note about what worked well in a particular session. That was the positivity piece. It was always interesting reading back, though, as sometimes I would be emotionally charged while writing. When I read it back, I would think that it sounded a bit negative and not how I wanted to feel or come across. It was useful to reflect in that way. It forced me to self-edit, to get it out of my head, out of my heart, and down on paper.

If you haven't started journaling already, give it a go and see if it helps. I think that once you start seeing and identifying with the words, the emotion or the sentiment, you can stop playing the event, or experience, back to yourself. I don't write every day at all, but during some of the more challenging periods in motherhood I've definitely relied on journaling, writing down what I'm thinking and feeling. I'll always try to add some notes on gratitude, too – what's going well, what, or who is making me feel good. That helps me to unlock my instinct, intuition and general sense about what I need to do to adapt and move forward during a difficult time.

Five ways to follow your instinct

You have everything you need inside you, here are some tips for unlocking it:

1. If you're not sure what to do, talk it out with a trusted friend for a fresh perspective.
2. Try journaling your thoughts to understand how you feel deep inside.
3. Rest your mind a moment, using a meditation app. Sometimes, the answer will land more clearly.
4. Know that following your instinct might cause a stir, but it doesn't mean that you shouldn't do it.
5. Trust your instinct. The more frequently the outcome is favourable, the stronger that trust becomes.

CHAPTER 5

Own Your Space

You wouldn't worry so much about what others think of you if you realised how seldom they do.

ELEANOR ROOSEVELT

Do you have a parent or a friend who compares you to others and spends a large proportion of any conversation telling you exactly what they think of what you're doing correctly – or not, as the case may be? Do you experience frequent comments that tend towards the critical, and instead of feeling uplifted as you wave your goodbyes or click off a phone call, you're left feeling attacked or subdued? This is a situation I know only too well. A couple of years ago a friend of mine seemed to feel duty bound to draw my attention to what was going on in social media, and essentially how everyone else was playing that game better than me. Every conversation would circle round to women that were working in sport and entertainment, highlighting how well they were doing, what partnership deals they had acquired, and other fabulous work opportunities that had come their way. Drawing direct comparisons to my life and other people's didn't seem to make sense to me, but as this type of questioning continued, I wondered what the endgame was.

Our long-standing friendship used to be rich with laughter and trading information. Sharing life concerns or trivial light-hearted banter, but now the nature of our dialogue filled me with dread, knowing that I would have to spend our phone calls listening to her challenge me about all the things I wasn't doing, and me defending myself and my lack of actions – in her opinion! Every conversation was a lecture with advice that I hadn't asked for. Was I being oversensitive? I'm all for receiving guidance and other people's opinions, but what do you do when conversations with friends repeatedly feel unhelpful and lean towards being negative to your emotional state? I would say that it's time to raise the red flag!

Two things happened when I reflected on how these exchanges made me feel. Firstly, I acknowledged that they were energy sapping and took me off my centre. They were not productive to me in the slightest. Secondly, I wondered whether the conversations were actually about me, or my friend's own feelings of significance and influence? Either way I felt I needed to lessen those negative interactions even if it meant sacrificing my friendship for a while. I remembered one of the most significant lessons I learned from being involved in athletics for so long: if you can't control what your competitors are going to do, you have to focus on what you *can* control.

Sometimes you may not be in the headspace to deal with confrontation, and I know at the time I had lots of other things going on, including a young child to nurture. Finding a coping strategy for me was, therefore, important, until a more appropriate time came along to deal with the issue head-on, which would then clear the air. Having your say is important if you value a friendship.

Adapt your social circle to make you happy

I'm a loyal friend, and I have some very long-lasting relationships, which I value dearly. Friendships change and can mature like a fine wine or turn sour, because people and their tolerance to certain behaviours change. Do your friendships need adapting?

Remember that the quirky characteristics you may turn a blind eye to in your twenties and thirties might become unattractive or unbearable in your forties and fifties. This could be because *you* have changed due to life experiences, and this is really OK. We are all allowed to move on and want different things.

A friendship shouldn't be one-sided, drain you or make you feel worse about yourself, so in the same way that you sort out your wardrobe once or twice a year, it might be useful to take stock and store certain friendships in the attic – keeping them safe, but not in everyday use.

Stepping back from people or situations that don't enhance your mental wellness shouldn't be selfish or unkind. See it as an act of kindness to yourself. How you do it might need some thought, however. Ghosting, ignoring or avoidance is not an ideal long-term strategy, but it might buy you time until you can deal with that relationship properly, especially if that relationship has played a major part in your life. I advocate sending a card, email or letter if you find direct conversations difficult.

Feeling good about yourself and surrounding yourself with positive vibrations is something you should not have to apologise for or compromise on. And if you are truly embracing adaptability, you might acquire new friendships or acquaintances because your interests, priorities and passions have changed. Be open to engage and share yourself and your time with new people. They may not become your forever friends, but they will boost your day-to-day life at the stage you are in, and they will help you to stay present and also to understand the phase of life you are in at the moment.

RUN YOUR OWN RACE

At most stages in my career there have been athletes who have shown bags of potential but never quite made it all the way, despite being talented juniors. These can be athletes who have shown impressive form in the lead-up to a big championship setting with personal bests in several events, but they never stand on a podium. One of my strengths was always to remain dialled into what I needed to do, focusing on my own progress, and quietly going about my own business. That strategy served me well as a sportswoman, and it still does to this day, in all aspects of my life. There's a great Jamaican proverb that was told to me by my great-grandmother, 'Payshent man ride donkey', translated as 'A patient man rides a donkey'. It means that we must exercise great patience to get to our goals. Let me help you stay focused on what you are doing, and not pay too much attention to what everyone else is up to; it will only slow you down and dim your inner sparkle.

Step into your power

Remember that you can own your own space when you:

- Stop getting distracted by other people's lives: you are on your own timeline – it's your life.
- Resist the temptation to compare yourself with others, from the school drop-offs to celebrity, and everything in between.
- Remember that everyone's life is nuanced and not always apparent or appropriate for you to

know about. It might not be as perfect as you imagine, or they (or others) might want to lead you to believe.

- Surround yourself with people who want to lift you, not drown you. Inspiration and feedback should feel positive, supportive and uplifting, if it doesn't make you feel good, it's not inspiration. And you don't have to listen to it.
- Acknowledge that you're in competition with only one person: the best version of yourself!

NO TIME FOR NEGATIVITY

In terms of *how* to deal with critics, naysayers and the constant comparers, that will depend on their personality type. Some will be instantly defensive, and telling them how they're making you feel will cause instant conflict. They might become very emotional and make it look as if you're the one at fault for expressing yourself and standing up for yourself. There's the potential for guilt-tripping: *I was only trying to help.*

Well, for me, it comes back to looking at your values, what's actually important and meaningful to you, as opposed to what is trendy right now, and making sure that outside influences aren't derailing you. I am going to tell you that this is a time when you do *not* have to adapt to anyone else's whims and demands; for example, in Chapter 1 I talked about the pressure that some people have put on me to post more on social media and why I have decided that it is not for me right now because of all the other roles that I have in my life. Posting and commenting on socials is low on my list of priorities. I know that for some people social media is a core of their business, and I fully respect that. But that's not my position.

If someone continues to criticise you, like my friend did me, you need to decide which comments are worthy of taking on board and adapting your life to include, and which ones you should ignore. I've spent a large portion of my adult life being critiqued, from athletics to my stint on *Strictly Come Dancing*, so I do have advice to share. In TV land, I am able to ask myself how the information I'm receiving makes me better, but when it's close interpersonal relationships at home or in the workplace, we can often feel personally attacked, depending on the tone of how something is said or written.

When I receive unasked-for feedback, I usually count to twenty, or reread something a couple of times, before reacting. In that very short processing time, I tend to think about what I have done to warrant the criticism. It's natural to want to defend yourself, which is what I have done many times in the past. In my deeper evaluation I mentally work from these three processes:

1. I look for examples where I have said or acted the way the person criticising suggests.
2. I consider if what's being said is not a reflection of me but of the person saying it.
3. I consider if that relationship is worth modifying my behaviour for.

There's a great quote that GB Olympic rowers have often used to do with performance, but I think that it can be applied here when thinking about being criticised, 'Will it make the boat faster?' Will it make you a better person to work with, be around, live with? Will it make you more aware of people's view of you? If it's a one-off comment, you might be better served by ignoring it and waiting to see if something similar comes up again in the future.

The situation with my friend that I am referring to made me feel that I had to second-guess myself. We have to ask ourselves why we attribute more weight to other people's opinions and expectations of us than our own – and often at the expense of our own well-being? I have always believed that there is room for us all, and we should lift each other up, not drag each other down. Women can be bad at this, worrying that there isn't room at the top or at the table for us all. This has to change. We need to learn how to tune out these external and internal negative voices in order to own our space and switch the narrative.

TUNE OUT UNHELPFUL COMPARISONS

After a disappointing turn of events in the 2004 Olympics, a journalist said to me, 'How does it feel to lose your crown as Queen of British athletics?' referring to Kelly Holmes, who had won double gold that year. I was taken aback. Why was he trying to make me feel inferior? Also, why could there only be one 'queen'? Sometimes you win, sometimes you lose. That's athletics, and it's also life. The way I saw it was that I had achieved the ultimate and I will always be an Olympic champion.

People's opinions can change about you very quickly, and that's why it's best not to absorb adulation or negativity. We see this highlighted perfectly when it comes to the England men's football team: one minute they're heroes, then the next they are vilified for missing a penalty. If you operate from the premise that you're somewhere in-between those spectrums, combined with deep introspection, you will maintain an honest view of yourself – not via other people's judgements. Don't be defined by others.

Kelly winning gold didn't define or downgrade me and my success – past or present. Someone else being invited to an event that I haven't been invited to doesn't need to be an issue. And the person who *makes* it an issue is the issue themselves. Sadly, as women, I think we are often pitted against one another and experience men trying to bring us down a peg or two. I had a work colleague who said that I needed to learn to enunciate better on TV. That was pretty hurtful. There was another sportswoman criticised for her accent during the last coverage of the Olympics. A man said on social media that it was 'jarring', causing a media storm. I have a big clash with these people. We should support, encourage and uplift. And look to spend time with people who want to do the same for us.

When not to adapt

Women, especially, often think that they have to adapt to fit in with everyone else and therefore take everyone else's opinions on board and change accordingly. But, you know, standing your ground is sometimes important. I don't have to change my behaviour or how I communicate on social media because my friend is obsessed to the point of weirdness with my career. Another example from my life is meeting another, new round of school parents. I don't necessarily want to immerse myself in that again – I have done it a lot with my other three kids, and I just don't have the time or desire any more. I am approachable, I am friendly, but it's not going to add anything to my life going to the parents' drinks. I used to think that I always had to toe the line and do what's expected or asked of me, but sometimes we've got to be clear: put yourself first and *know* yourself clearly. It's OK to step back. You don't have to adapt to other people's expectations. Sometimes they can do the shift work.

- Be clear about what you can and can't do. You don't need to make excuses.
- Don't allow the pressure of expectation to perform in a certain way get to you. Stand strong.
- Give yourself permission to *not* be drawn into everything. Put your peace first. Shut out the drama.
- Often in our teens, twenties and thirties, we're looking for that sense of belonging. Wise up. Today, you choose the communities and the

spaces that you dwell in and occupy; focus on what feeds your soul. You don't need to morph into someone you're not. Individuality is cool.

THERE IS ONLY ONE YOU

A friend of mine told me recently that she had tried to dumb down her very posh accent (her words, not mine) when she went to university outside London. She'd never been so acutely aware of how she sounded, as she'd been surrounded by people who sounded like her all her life until that point, and it made her uncomfortable. Conversely, my husband talks about how he used to get so fed up with people asking him to repeat himself when he moved from Liverpool to London that he worked hard on softening his accent. He sounds like a Cockney these days. Granted, society has become much more tolerant of difference, and powerful conversations around diversity have helped to turn the dial and raise awareness for many. We have also become more acutely sensitive as to how intersectionality impacts individuals and can result in them feeling excluded, but there's still work to be done.

Being a woman of colour, and an only child from a

single-parent family, I've often felt a little different, so it comes as no surprise to me that in many of my circles, post my athletics career, I stand out – representing the minority with my ethnicity and gender. I have had conflicting feelings about this from time to time. I think that when you're in the public domain you are permitted into spaces that would possibly be off-limits or questioned if your reputation hadn't opened what would be seen as a closed shop.

My heritage makes me *me*, but I also sometimes want to feel that I belong and fit in without having to make so much effort. I remember being at secondary school, being the sportiest girl, and going up to receive awards and recognition. Part of me didn't want to stand out then, and sometimes I still don't want to now. But I've grown to embrace the uniqueness of who I am. And I urge you to embrace *your* uniqueness, too. Instead of concentrating on the negative aspects – who you are not or what you don't have – allow yourself to think about the strides you have made and the impact that you have had. I try to do this and think of the impact that I have made on other women, other mothers, and on female sports pundits of colour.

Look in the mirror, what do you see?

- When you are the only female or the only non-white person on your team, how does that make you feel?

- Do you have the coping strategies to allow you to bring your best self to work? Almost certainly, at the start of a new job, you'll have a heightened awareness of the differences and similarities you have with your colleagues.

- We all want to fit in and we need a sense of belonging. If you don't feel you belong, at the start, look for the connectors. Who are the people who seem open to engaging with you? Focus your attention there.

- Look for the things you do have in common, not just for the ways you're different. It might be that you have a shared work ethic, that your creative process is similar or that you are juggling similarly competing demands.

- And ask yourself what you're willing to do to blend in. Will you choose to not wear lipstick, or to wear your hair a certain way, in order to feel accepted? Or perhaps you'll keep your attire simple, with

> clean lines, and wear trouser suits to align with your male counterparts. It's OK to want to blend in, but don't lose yourself entirely.

FIND FLEXIBILITY WHILE STAYING TRUE TO YOURSELF

There have been many occasions over the past decade when I've asked myself who the real Denise Lewis is: *Who am I, when so much of my time goes into supporting my husband and kids and developing my career?* To add to that, when you're in the public eye, there's an expectation that you'll always be available, upbeat, friendly and accommodating. I've had to learn that sometimes it's like being a chameleon, adapting to the environment. The more skilled you become at this and the more you recognise your own personal boundaries, the easier it will be to switch off when you need to, confident that you can make the right adaptations at the right moment to protect your peace. If you always feel as if you have your game face on, disguising your true identity from the world, you might be left feeling exposed and exhausted.

*

How can we stay true to ourselves and our identity, while also fitting in and adapting to different environments? I have already touched upon this in Chapter 1, but what I've realised over the years is that comparison slows you down. Let's take a very literal example, here. You're about to take off in a race and your opponents are getting into position on either side of you. Now, you could focus your attention on one of them, check what she's doing, how she's looking – but then the gun is fired and she shoots off while you're still getting into position. Alternatively, you can stay in your lane. Eyes focused ahead of you, ready to take off yourself. This example can be used across all aspects of life, and the result is the same: comparing yourself to the people around you will not get you to where you want to go, but staying focused on your own path will do. Keep a sharp focus on your own goals, while motivating others when asked for your advice. I may have spent many years competing in a solo event, but I'm still very much a team player. I want to rise, and I want to help others rise with me. That means working out what I need to do to get there, focusing on my journey and then teaching others how I made it there. I hope this book helps with that mission.

SET YOUR OWN GOALS

I was not overly aware of being a young black girl when I was a child, because I grew up in a multicultural environment and at school, and I didn't feel that my race or ethnicity held me back at all. It wasn't until much later that I became aware of the prejudices that being black and a girl is met with. I saw my mum working hard and managing to achieve what she wanted – for herself and for me. And I saw my grandmother, too, who worked hard but took long holidays in Jamaica and travelled to Hawaii, the Canary Islands and many more amazing places. My mum and Nan showed me that hard work affords you a better life. I used to jokingly say to my mum, 'You live to work,' and she'd reply, very earnestly, 'No, I work because I have to.'

I don't remember comparing myself to my peers unfavourably, because what I saw is that if you are clear on your goals – such as my mum moving to a nicer neighbourhood – you can work hard and achieve them. It didn't feel as if anything was off-limits. Now, I tell my kids that they can be anything they want if they put in the work. Sometimes it falls on deaf ears, but I hope it's penetrating.

As a family, and through the generations, this is what we teach the younger lot: own your life, reach for what it is that you want, and please don't worry about what others are doing. Someone else's success doesn't dictate yours; you dictate that yourself. No, you can't ever predict whether that dream will come true, you can only hold on to it, work towards it, become more resilient and keep going – there's more hope of it coming true if you do all that. Of course, talent comes into it and this informs your potential, but there is a point at which the work ethic and persistence of doing the right thing takes over. It's about being able to take on advice, listen, execute, and overcome physical and mental challenges; plus, know that you are going to receive negative criticism and process that in a way that makes you more resilient.

I think that once you realise that it's not about looking to your left and right, regarding your peers or competition, but it's about looking ahead: that's when you really start to fly. Rather than wondering why things felt hard at times and deciding to just give it all up, you should think: *What is this test? What am I being tested for on this one? How am I supposed to respond? How am I supposed to feel about this? What's the learning here?* I was always looking, and I still am, for ways to better myself. I stayed centred on me, Denise Lewis, what I wanted and how I was going to make it happen. That's my wish for you, too. Set your own goals.

There will always be tests on your resolve from the universe, if you like. When I was growing up, there wasn't much money, so if I lost my bus pass, I would be forced to walk for the rest of the month, until my mum could buy the next one. I once lost it on week two of the month, and I walked to school every day for two weeks – it was a 45-minute walk. I must have loathed her then because it was a real low point. And I think I might have been fractionally late every day. I had no one else to blame but myself. It was a test, and I got through it. It wasn't a question of: *Why can't my mum just replace my bus pass?* Those thoughts didn't occur to me. I made a mistake, I learned from it. I didn't look around for anyone else to blame or make things better.

 Look back at how you dealt with your goals

Make a note of your answers to the following:

1. How did your childhood impact the future goals you set for yourself?
2. Were there moments, growing up, when you compared yourself to others?
3. If yes, how did you continue, in spite of those comparisons?
4. Do you compare yourself to your peers, now?
5. If yes, how would it feel to let go of all comparison and focus just on your own life?

WITH A LITTLE HELP FROM MY FRIENDS

We all need people in our corner, though, who see our potential and help us to see it, too. You need validation from somewhere; somebody affirming what they can see. There have been various people doing that for me along the way, keeping me in the game. I've had help from friends, coaches, and sometimes, it comes from places I had least expected it to. It's not always the obvious person. It could be the postman who's been watching your career and says, 'I always knew you could do it', or 'You're really doing an amazing job.' These little signs are out there.

You've got your part to play and your role to deliver on, but people who encourage you – and see things that you don't see in yourself – help you to keep rising. When you can marry self-esteem with a positive comment and action from someone whose opinion matters and is valid, you're off to the races. It keeps you going. You can't always be galloping; the repetitive parts of life can force you to trot or canter on occasion, but a boosting word from someone you value can get you galloping again. Search for those runners and riders.

HOW TO RAISE YOUR SELF-ESTEEM

I definitely experienced low, or at least fluctuating, self-esteem in my teenage years. I was a performer as a child, I loved singing and dancing, but then, in my teens, I got a little shy. I started to feel self-conscious about how I looked. Girls in my year started to have conversations about boyfriends and beauty, which worried and confused me a little. I never felt like the belle of the ball at that age – I used to have a little bit of eczema on my knees. Perhaps a lot of teens feel self-conscious in a similar way: that you're different from your friends in some ways, and that being different isn't a good thing.

My mum was working in the care system, in nursing homes, and then for the Post Office at night to supplement her income during my mid-teens, so I only saw her fleetingly. She'd wake up and I would see her in the mornings as she was preparing to leave, then she'd come home at about 5pm, cook dinner, get washed and changed, and then be off to job number two through the night, come back at the crack of dawn, wash, have breakfast, then go to sleep and be up again when I was getting ready for school. It was punishing. Although I say don't compare yourself to others, I do remember saying to myself at one stage: *I do not want that life for myself.*

My self-esteem was tested in those years, but I knew I wanted more than that – and somewhere deep down I knew I could do it. My athletics training was about working towards something different from what my mum had, a life that would enable me to see the world, but as my school grades began to slip, I started to feel unsure of myself. I wondered if I was meant to be going to university or out to work, and it wasn't clear-cut for me. Other people around me seemed to have a distinct pathway in front of them – and I did, with athletics – but I was having to work out if that was the best trajectory, especially during periods when I wasn't getting the results I wanted to be achieving in competitions, and my self-esteem was taking a knock.

Perhaps the largest knock to my self-esteem was when I was competing at the Athens Olympics, which, as I've shared in a previous chapter, was a disaster. It was truly painful for me not to be able to compete and defend my title, as well as feeling out of sorts and not capable or fit enough to perform. I left Athens feeling really dejected and very low. I didn't come out of my room for days, and people were asking if I was OK. Somehow, I regained my composure. A couple of my friends knew that I was in a bad way, so they took me out to eat in Kensington. We sat, and they licked my wounds and let me lick my wounds, and we talked, and they made me laugh.

I let go of what I thought I wanted to be doing, or should be doing, and – as you know – I threw myself into *Strictly*. I knew that it was going to be several weeks of something pleasurable. I love dancing, and I decided to see it as an opportunity. And it was a lifeline, because I shut the whole athletic feeling away and just took on this role. I had the best dance partner you could have wished for, Ian Waite. And he was just so much fun to be around. I loved the experience. I loved changing my hat to become a dancer for weeks on end. Those live shows satisfied the competitor in me, and because we were training every single day, I had a reason to get out of bed in the morning, plus having some fun each day, as well as someone holding my hand. It was very bonding, and a great boost to my sagging self-esteem at a dark time.

 Choose something different
(it can boost your self-esteem)

Make a note of your answers to the following:

1. When have you gone against the grain and done something unexpected?
2. How did it feel to do it?
3. Right now, is there any 'wild card' you would like to play that could boost your self-esteem?
4. What's stopping you from doing it?
5. If you were to do it, what might change? Do you think it would have a positive effect on your self-esteem?

Although it's a different arena from athletics, *Strictly* still requires the same sort of mental rehearsals. There are no edits. If you fall, you fall on national television, which is the same as in the athletic arena. There are parallels. A part of me was thinking that I shouldn't take it too seriously, but at the same time, there was no turning off that competitor in me. I thought: *If I'm going to do it, I'm going to do it well.* If I was investing time and effort, I wanted to go as far as possible, boosting my self-esteem every step of the way. But I also knew that in TV land, the result isn't always in your control, so I controlled what I could, which was my performance and the energy that I put into rehearsals.

I managed to control my nerves during the live performance, which I think was a real asset. I was a competitor in an arena, and I came alive – who wouldn't? It was fusing all my passions. I love make-up, I love music, I love to dance and I love to perform. It was so important for my morale and my confidence at that time. Also, I was reconnecting with that child self that I had left behind, who wanted to dance but made other choices. I got an opportunity, later in life, to express myself in that way. It was just fantastic.

When your performance is being dissected by the judges, it does feel really personal. But having spent my life up to that point with coaches who would be telling me how I could improve, I was OK with receiving that information for my betterment. I've always been able to take that on board and use it to improve. If you feel your own self-esteem waiver, look outside the places you usually source it, and adapt your days to find the little boosts and glimmers of self-esteem somewhere else: with friends, by taking a solo trip abroad, or by trying a new hobby – as I did with *Strictly*. Try not to put all your self-esteem eggs in only one basket; know that you are more than just one thing.

COMPARISON IN MOTHERHOOD

If there's ever a time when comparing yourself to others becomes overwhelming, it's motherhood. We all enter it without much knowledge of what we're meant to be doing and we have to learn along the way, which leaves us vulnerable to judgement and comparison. But now that I'm four kids – and well over twenty years – into parenthood, I take other parents' comparisons and criticisms with a pinch of salt. Usually, I just think: *Oh, that belongs to you.* And I don't adopt it or let it influence my parenting, because each household has to have its own sense of what it's about. The dynamics are so different in every home. I want you to feel that you have permission to mummy your way, adapting your family into a shape that makes you *all* happy and healthy. I think one particularly tough comparison for parents is looking at another family and seeing their kid is doing every activity from Monday to Sunday, seemingly excelling at them all, and feeling somewhat *less than* if their child isn't. Stop it. You don't know what really goes on in that household. Make the decisions for *your* family, and do whatever is going to work for you.

I haven't gone into the parenting process with a conscious plan of action. It's been borne out of what I believe to be good values, picked up from my world travels, following a North Star or my heart towards what feels right. Peer pressure – another word for comparison, really – is often greater for young people, because they don't always have that same North Star that adults do – that is, knowing who they are yet. The adaptability piece, in terms of raising children and not getting distracted by what others are doing, involves getting a firm understanding of what's going on around you, and being conscious and open-minded about the world in which your children live. It requires scheduling time together; if I'm not actually having quality time with my children, I become reactive to their behaviour. When you're busy, that becomes harder to do, but time together, to reset, to appreciate each other, is a must.

I've mothered in the best way I know how. I've been at home when they got back from school to help them with their homework and make sure that it's done. I've been there to chauffeur them to activities. I've moved them to different schools, if I thought that would help them to thrive. But I've also been working. I haven't been that mum who's at home baking and doing yoga and having coffee mornings. We mothers need to think about what works for our family and ourselves, unperturbed or not thrown off course by external opinions or comments. There should be no comparisons, only compassion. As I've said before, being a mum is the hardest job in the world. We women must remember that our different identities can coexist. It's hard, but it's worth fighting for; however, it's not about looking left and right, and seeing if other people's kids are better disciplined than yours, winning more races at sports day, or doing chores without being asked, it's about working out a solution for your family that will suit everyone – and sticking to it.

 Best mum in the world . . .
for your kids

In your role as a parent you might feel lesser, or run ragged, or confused at times, but your child wouldn't swap you for the world. Concentrate on what you're getting right for a minute, write down the answers to these questions, and be proud:

1. Note down three things you're really good at doing as a mother. Perhaps you're caring, organised, gentle or calm.

2. Also note down one thing you'd like to be better at, and why?

3. Who do you compare yourself to as a mother? Get clear on why you make this comparison.

4. Journal around what change you could make in your own life to remove the need for comparison.

5. Note down three things your kids have said to you in the last week that made you happy and boosted your self-esteem.

OTHER PEOPLE'S PERCEPTIONS OF YOU

When I look back at my mum and her journey, she's the embodiment of striding out and striding through very unsettled and turbulent waters. She had that inner drive and determination. She's never been in debt (except for her mortgage), she manages her funds and she's accepting of her situation. But she was not accepting of the stereotypes that may have been put on her, about being a single parent who will claim everything she can. No, she has worked – and is still working – and doing as much as she can to move herself forward.

A crucial element, in terms of owning your space, is not letting other people's perceptions of who you are and what you're capable of bring you down in any way. We've talked about how there were people boosting and validating me, but there were also people who couldn't handle me finding certain successes, because of what I looked like and where I was from. There were opportunities that weren't afforded to me, because the system wasn't quite ready for either a black female or someone coming from sports to be stepping out of their box into TV. It's other people not being ready for change, or for something different, that has limited the world of sports. Even now, we're still not seeing many female pundits commentating on the men's games with authority and knowledge and opinion. If they do, it receives a lot of backlash.

Corporations and businesses are recognising the need for change, seeing how the landscape has already changed, but still there is a lot of resistance. As a black woman, I've always had to be dogged, standing my ground and improving quicker than everyone else, in order for people to see me. I've also had to bring an energy to whatever environment I'm in to gain people's trust, in their space. It's about likeability. I bring light and connectivity, and I try to connect with people. Men don't have to bring all that;

they just arrive as they are. They believe they have a right to be there. But when you're from a minority group, you have to access your 'softer skills' that endear you to an audience or endear you to people making the decisions. I think our male counterparts have relied on the fact that they are men, and men make the decisions, so there's that instantaneous connection. Not all men, but many, could still do better when it comes to accessing their softer skills.

As I said earlier, though, having people backing you in your corner, and championing you, is crucial. It's a gift that enables people to flourish and to believe in themselves and their capabilities. And so, the essence for me in everything that I do is: *How can I give that back?* I feel blessed to have been supported in the ways that I have, and now I want to pay forward that energy and motivation to others. Whether that's individuals, children, companies, organisations, the boards I serve on, it's all about the same thing for me: *Can I contribute? Can I play my part?* Having success in my sport allowed me to champion myself, and now I'm adapting that spirit to enjoy championing others.

Still, when I'm hosting or at certain events, I'm often the only black woman in the room. I decide that I will be the best representation of my community and the communities that I serve. Womanhood is integral and central to that, as is my ethnicity. When I do it, I do it with gusto. It's about how I present myself and how I interact with people. There's always a learning opportunity and a teaching opportunity, and I try to impart something that people will take away, thinking it was interesting, or not what they were expecting. We can't assume that everyone has grown up with or has had someone of colour within their social circle or community. Therefore, I feel in my various roles I'm a representative for people of colour and I want to perform my roles well, hoping it can dislodge people's unconscious biases and potentially loosen up any preconceived ideas that may exist or have been taught, eventually leading to seeing difference in a positive way.

Retiring can be hard: saying goodbye to a huge chunk of your life – something that defined you, something that gave you a reason for waking up in the morning. You have an idea that there will be a massive void; a hole that you'll never be able to fill. And, no, life won't be the same. It just won't. But I've made it my mission to prove that it can still be good, and it's up to me to keep that momentum going. I've had to seek other joys and other highs, and I have had some equally high moments since winning that gold medal. Being something of a change-maker, in terms of representation, does that for me, helping other people to shift and adapt their biases for a better world. Find that thing that is unique to you, that boosts your self-esteem while boosting others, and go for it. You can do it. And remember, you're only in competition with yourself.

Challenge people's perceptions of you

Make a note of your answers to the following:

1. Do you ever worry about people's perception of you?
2. Are there times when you put yourself forward, even though people might not have expected you to?
3. If not, what space would you like to occupy that you don't already?
4. Who can support you with that?
5. If you're going through a life transition, how do you confidently move into this new arena?

OWN THE MENOPAUSE

Getting older feels like a blessing, and so I'm curious, rather than concerned, about how it will feel to be moving through the menopause. This is a time when women can be made to feel unimportant, as if their worth is decreasing, but similar to all aspects of womanhood, there can be great power in moving through this next life stage.

Five years ago, I had some hot flushes. I thought it must be the menopause, and then I realised that I was actually pregnant with Troy. Since then, I've had the occasional hot flush combined with that feeling of it taking over, but perhaps only twice in the last couple of years and then they disappeared. It caught me unawares when it happened, though, because there was no precursor just: *boom*, heat in the face and in the body – and then it goes. You wonder what on earth just happened. The good news is that the medical community and media are adapting rapidly to our questions and concerns about the menopause, and there's enough information out there for us to feel supported and make informed decisions about how we'll move through it today.

I'm not currently experiencing symptoms, such as perspiring, which I know can be very embarrassing for some women. I have friends who when experiencing a hot flush look as if they've just stepped out of a shower, and so they are not able to commit fully to environments that will raise their body temperature. If they're going to a bar or clubbing, they have to have a fan at hand. There's also the possibility of slipping into anxiety or hot flushes at night. These things are real and happening to women around me, and the general consensus among my peers is that it is best to do something about it before it hits you. Adapt your life to this new hormonal roller coaster before it takes you for the ride you don't want to be on. I've got friends who are menopause ambassadors, and they're championing the use of HRT, whereas other women would prefer to go about it in their own way. Adapt your midlife to the way that works for you; my one interjection would be to exercise when you can – I truly believe that helps everything.

 Manage the menopause

If you are at this life stage, make a note of your answers to the following:

1. How do you feel about getting older, as a woman?
2. What menopause symptoms have you found the most difficult?
3. Do you have other women friends who are also going through it, to give you support and solidarity?
4. Can you identify something empowering about the menopause?
5. What would improve this life stage for you?

You know what? When you feel good in your heart, body, mind and soul, you don't need to compare yourself to anyone else. I truly believe that you're as young as you feel, whatever your age, and if you don't feel young, change that: move more, eat better, sleep more, stress less. My philosophy is that limitations shouldn't be imposed on your physical abilities by others, or what people have told you about yourself, but you have to be willing to do the mental homework, which is quite simply: be more positive and be adaptive to whatever stage of life you're in. We're not all born with bags of confidence, waking up each morning like Jim Carey's character in *The Mask* and saying to the awaiting world, 'Somebody stop me!' If only! But you *can* start with thinking about all that you have to be grateful for – that will get you in a positive mindset – and then work towards letting that positivity seep into all areas of your life. Tell yourself who you are *and* who you want to become, own your identity *and* your goals. Don't let someone else tell you how your life should look. Own your pace, own your space, own your mind.

Five ways to own your space

1. Look around you and decide what you'd like to do differently.

2. From that point onward, don't compare. Stay in your own lane.

3. Remember that other people's lives are not your life; there are lots of elements and aspects that we don't see.

4. Be confident in your choices, and if something isn't working, change it.

5. Adapt to each life stage, including motherhood and menopause, while maintaining your key values: don't fight it, embrace it – and keep being uniquely, wonderfully you. Nobody does it better.

CHAPTER 6

Let Go and Seek Support

Asking for help isn't a sign of weakness, it's
a sign of strength. It shows that you have
the courage to admit when you don't know
something, and to learn something new.

BARACK OBAMA

There are times in life when you can survive on sheer
willpower, gut instinct and determination, and there are
times when you need to let go of some of the control you're
clinging on to, and ask for help. Some circumstances will
be beyond your control, and you'll need to rely on people
to help you navigate them, showing you methods to adapt
to turbulent times that you had never considered. In my

athletics career, although I relied on many people to help me – coach, nutritionist, physio – I always knew where I was heading and I chose people who could help me get there. It's been motherhood – the biggest adaptation of my life – that required me to dig deep into myself *and* reach out for support from others.

There is a magic to motherhood, and I find it fascinating how these babies turn into little people. Yes, they may get on my nerves, but they're good people.

That doesn't mean it's been easy, however – on the contrary. The last eight years, raising my children as they've become teenagers, have been really tough, and working with my neurodivergent children is also a new thing for me that I've had to adapt my parenting to. I've been to places that I never thought I would be able to go to as a parent, and there is no preparation for that. There is no amount of training or life experience that can prepare you for when one of your children is not coping and functioning well. But I'm learning and changing how I do things; for example, I now understand that Lauryn needs time to process situations and change expectations. I've stopped us being such a busy family, rushing around, because *that* didn't work for her. She needs more notice, much more tolerance and understanding. Adapting our schedule to allow for what she needs has made our house function so much more smoothly.

Help yourself, then ask for help

When you're in a state of panic, whether at work or on a playdate with your child, it's hard to order your thoughts. You need a clear plan of action in an emergency, and you'll probably need to call others in to help. But first, centre yourself. Do a grounding breathing exercise, breathing in through your nose for a count of five and out for ten. Releasing more carbon dioxide should help to calm your nerves. It might feel counterintuitive to be doing a breathing exercise during a crisis, but actually you need to be able to think straight. Focus on your breath, perhaps do five rounds like this, and you might notice that solutions drop into your mind as you do it. Either way, you'll return to the room with a clearer mind to work with others as you decide what needs to happen, and when, to resolve the situation.

GET HELP AROUND THE HOUSE

What is a woman to do when the people she shares her home with seem unwilling to adapt – even when it's the right thing to do? Every household has its own dynamics, and so you have to learn about yours and your partner's, and be flexible enough to meet in the middle. In those early stages of dating, you were probably not having conversations about what your mum and dad contributed within the home, what the kitchen looked like before you went to bed each night, and so on. It's not exactly romantic chatter, is it? But it always comes later, once things start to feel lopsided and you're trying to work out why someone isn't contributing as you'd like them to. To break the cycle of it all falling to women, we've got to educate our boys from a very early age.

In the last few years, I've been trying to stop doing chores in the evening at a certain point because I can get too carried away with it. Instead, I try to relax. I'm on the go all day, but previously I was then also working into the night, putting on a wash, clearing stuff away, or pairing socks, and I would never rest except when I was in bed. It's so important to have downtime other than when you're sleeping or binge-watching *Bridgerton* or listening to a podcast in the bath. You need time to just *be*.

This is what we all need to get better at learning: be clear on what you're willing to do, willing to let go of, willing to ask for help with, and *not* willing to let go of. Don't forget to check in with yourself about your own needs. We have to check in. And it's a *must* not only for your own sense of self but also for your family unit and your career. You can't do it all alone. You need help. And remember, when your family unloads the dishwasher or puts the washing away, they are not doing you a favour, you should not be overly grateful. You are a team. Everyone needs to adapt to a way that works for you all at home. We need to do this as individuals, and as families. When you're starting to fail or feel as if you're unravelling a little bit, it's because you haven't done that very important piece, which is just checking back and checking in. It's your mental MOT.

---

 take stock for help around the house

Make a note of your answers to the following:

1. What jobs do you do around the house? List them all – whether physical or mental chores you deal with for everyone in your family.
2. What would you like more help with?
3. Who could you ask?
4. How would it feel to get one task off your list?
5. How often do you check in with the people you live with?

---

6. If you have a partner, sit together and ask yourselves how you both feel about these questions: are we doing enough together as a couple to feel as if we are moving forward or are we stagnating? How could we help each other more to make everyone's lives easier?

SUPPORTIVE SPOUSES

There was a period in my marriage when things felt incredibly challenging. I wasn't getting what I needed, and not just with the chores or childcare, but in the way we treated each other. Steve was going off to play tennis and golf and not coming back on time. It felt as if there wasn't any accountability for him and his role; meanwhile, I was doing all the self-sacrificing. Perhaps it looked to him as if I was having downtime going out to various sports or entertainment parties, shows or events, but these weren't social occasions, they were work. Getting ready for the red carpet might seem glamorous, but it's actually really stressful. You're worried that you don't look good enough, wondering if your hair and dress will hold up to scrutiny, and whether the media will print a bad photo of you the next day. I needed *actual* downtime. And because I wasn't getting it, I started burning out. I couldn't cope with that work–mum juggle any more. We had bits of childcare here and there, but not nearly enough.

It got to the point where I thought: *I chose this life, but not the burnout. I never thought it would be so heavily weighted in one direction.*

Around 2015, I realised that I needed external help and support. I was feeling overburdened. I was travelling for work, and each time I returned home, the house would be in a state of chaos and mess, which led to a power struggle between myself, Steve and the kids. While I was trying to build my career, he'd taken on new ventures – he's an entrepreneur – which called on his time. Plus, working in music management means that he's taking phone calls through the night, as he has to look after his colleagues and clients. It became too much, so we had counselling together to understand the fundamental issues and how to navigate them. You should never feel ashamed about getting therapy – sometimes, with a neutral third person present, it's the only space you have to share problems without things descending into the same old argument.

The primary lesson we learned was that we needed to create more time in our schedules for us as a couple. But that can be hard when time isn't your friend, but we both made an effort to adapt our calendars to make that work.

We also learned that when both people in the couple are exhausted, things fly out of your mouth without thinking and if it's aggressive, or sounds accusatory, that's it: you're in argument territory. It's met with the same energy. The key, we found, was to feel our way into challenges, thinking more carefully about what we wanted to say rather than going straight in with the attack. It's about avoiding conflict; for example, when my husband says, 'I'll be back at 8.30pm' and then rocks up at 11pm, I can say, 'Oh, three hours late then?' And get all snarky. Or I can go in more gently, with my feelings, something like, 'When you come back late, I don't know if you're OK, and it makes me feel worried. Please can you call to tell me you're going to be late next time.'

If you want to live harmoniously, or with fewer ups and downs at least, you've got to do the work, both of you, and sometimes get help from an external source – be it a babysitter so that you can have date nights, or a marriage-guidance counsellor. We all come into a relationship with learned behaviours and habits, so knowing yourself – and your past influences – better will help you to adapt what you can to fit better into the new home life you're trying to create. Help yourself as you help others.

Five ways to let go and ask for help

1. Identify who the people are you could rely on in an emergency.
2. Trust your instinct about the process you need to go through to find a solution.
3. Remember that people are often very willing to help out – you're not alone.
4. Within the home, every family member can play a role – it's not all down to the mother.
5. Identify your needs, your capability and your capacity. State those needs.

CHAPTER 7

Find Inner Strength and Peace

Nothing can dim the light which shines from within.

MAYA ANGELOU

There will be times in life that test you; moments that make you want to shout and scream – and, honestly, my advice would be to do just that. Sometimes, there's nothing like letting it all go if you need to cry, or scream into your pillow, or get in your car on your own and belt out a fight song at the top of your voice with the windows down. Just do it! The worst thing we can do to ourselves is to bottle up emotions that need to come out. Some tough times will make you want to shrink into yourself, weakened and vulnerable; in those times, if you need to walk out of a certain environment or leave the situation that has caused a barrage of upsetting moments, do it. The worst thing you can do is stay stuck, glued to the spot, feeling more and more emotional and exposed. My antidote to these understandable fight-or-flight emotions is this: when you get a chance to replenish those negative feelings with positive energy, do so!

Remember in the first chapter we spoke about self-soothing? I'm not a naturally calm person. I don't think of myself as flappable, but I get irritated by rudeness, people who walk without looking where they're going because they are staring down at their phone, inconsiderate parking – and many more things besides! I was extremely calm and level-headed as an athlete, but in real life, staying calm and carrying on is a bigger challenge for me.

A few years ago, I started having panic attacks at night. Looking back, I know it was caused by problems in my marriage, but at the time I was concerned that something was wrong with me or I had developed sleep apnoea. It went away after a few months but returned once again during another period of heavy conflict between my husband and myself. Because of the disturbed sleep, I woke up very groggy in the mornings, but I still had to perform the school run and get on with my day. I'm not the type of person to sit down and take five in the afternoon, but there were moments when I would find myself drifting off to sleep while sitting and watching *Go Jetters* with Troy around 4.30pm after picking him up from nursery.

The fear and dread that crept up inside me at night at the thought of another panic attack was awful. I left the TV on as a distraction and drank warm milk to comfort myself like my mum made for me when I was a child, but as soon as the lights went out, *BAM!* I was on my feet scrambling to get to the window to see outside, or opening the window for fresh air. I propped my pillow up like one would in hospital, to sleep more upright. These things helped a bit, but my issues came to a head in 2021, when I was working in Salford for BBC Sport. The hotel we usually stayed in is compact and you can't open the windows. I hadn't anticipated that I would have problems, because the panic attacks were random and not every night. But, sure enough, the night before the World Indoor Championships, those scary familiar feelings started to gather momentum inside me. I paced the room until my breathing had calmed, put the reading light on, sat on the bed, paced some more, put music on – I had strong urges to walk along the corridor, but the embarrassment of someone seeing me was too much to bear. The night ticked on – 2am, 4am – and I had to be up at 6.30am and do eight hours of live television. I wanted to cry, scared that I was losing it, that my troubles at home would creep into my ability to be professional at work.

It's moments like that when you have to dig deep and focus your mind on transitioning out of your emotions and adapting your mood to what is required to perform. I've found that the more you indulge in negative chatter with yourself – or others – the more you will compound the problem, causing more mental fatigue, and making getting and staying asleep even harder. Somehow, I managed to get through the next three days of live TV coverage, but I knew that I had to do something proactively to mitigate the chances of something like this happening again at work. I sincerely believe that we all have a serene side to us; sometimes we just need to adapt how we look at problems to activate it. I'm now going to tell you how I have changed my responses to things to activate mine.

HOW TO ADAPT YOUR SCHEDULE TO REDUCE STRESS

When time seems to be spiralling away from me, and there's a sense that my days have just been filled with stuff that I can't even recall, and I haven't hit my workout and food goals, it won't be long until I feel tension just sitting in my body. At that point, I know that I've taken on too much and that the scales have tipped unfavourably because I haven't been honouring my intrinsic self. I have the luxury, to some degree, of being able to alter my weekly schedule. This is one of the pluses of being self-employed, I guess. Irrespective of your working situation, when tension and irritability, fatigue and bad habits creep in, these are signs that you are not making time for yourself, and it would be advisable to redress this as soon as you can.

Try:

- Self-soothing. Find a calming physical anchor that you might benefit from; for example, perhaps your soother could be a familiar blanket, a favourite teapot, your bed, a specific collection of books you own, a drawer in the fridge that is just for treats and so on.
- Walking, listening to music – choose a favourite track from the era when you felt carefree.
- Taking a bath or shower with a few drops of essential oils (my go-to is ylang-ylang).
- Going to bed. When I feel emotional or overwhelmed, my first retreat is to my bed to be still, cry a bit, then sleep. It's the body's natural way to heal and repair itself. When someone has experienced massive body trauma, it's not uncommon for them to be placed in an induced coma in the ICU; when we have a temperature or are unwell, the first thing

our body tells us is to seek rest and sleep. All the signs are there if we stop and think about them – the function of sleep is so much more than just sleep.

- Burning fig-scented candles (the fragrance reminds me of outdoors) and being still for as long as I need/can afford, lying down and taking slow, deep breaths.
- The sound of nature. It has an instant calming effect – I feel most relaxed when I can hear water, whether it's a babbling brook or the crashing of waves – and walking in green spaces has that same effect on my spirit; a deep connection that I find very soothing. According to philosophy, our universe is made up of four classic elements: earth, water, fire and air, so it shouldn't be surprising that humans get replenished by being exposed to these natural wonders in the form of sea, sun, green spaces and fresh air. If you can't access these natural areas, there are a number of relaxing sounds that you can find on YouTube, for example.

POSITIVITY AND OPTIMISM

I've always thought of myself as a realist. I don't walk around wearing rose-tinted glasses by any means. But I'm also an optimist who is always looking up and thinking: *What's next, what else is there?* knowing that there's still another mountain I can climb. I'm a big believer that if you are prepared to look up, look out to the sides a little bit, you'll find things, you'll uncover ideas, you'll discover opportunities. It's from that secure footing that I find my inner strength and calm. After all, most of the time, if you believe that it can happen, you'll find the strength to continue through any storms that might arise until you reach a calm after the storm. I like to give things a go, to see how I can help with a problem or a situation, find a route and a strategy. That's probably the Olympic athlete in me: you set out a programme, you develop physically and mentally in tandem, and when you recognise that something isn't working, you look within yourself to see what it is that you need in order to be better.

Being a positive person helps, too. Not only do I believe that it's always possible to do more and be better but I also like to take a positive energy with me wherever I go, enthusiastically imparting it to others. I'll say, 'Have you thought about this? Is there a way that you can unlock this side or potential in you, or use this option? Have you explored it?' Then if they're responsive, be it one of my teenagers or a fellow athlete, my thinking goes granular: 'What are the finer details? What are the layers we need to work through? What needs to happen at each step of the way?'

Working towards becoming an Olympic champion required hard work, effort, determination, perseverance and self-belief, but really it was a one-dimensional challenge. I knew where I was heading. I got my place on the Olympic podium, holding my gold medal to my lips, and I felt as if I was in my power. But, actually, life since then has required much more in terms of inner strength and calm than during that period. I've had to adapt, learn how to mother four very different children, navigate marriage, hold on to my friendships, continue with my career and make sure that I'm looking after myself while looking after so many others. There are so many layers to life, once you've moved beyond your goal. The key to balancing it all is often to keep calm.

 Choose positivity and optimism

Make a note of your answers to the following:

1. Write down three things that you feel hopeful about.
2. What change would you like to see in your life that others might not believe is possible but you know is?

3. How can you spread more positivity, starting today?
4. What opportunities lie ahead for you?
5. What opportunities would you like to bring to fruition?

THE CALMING POWER OF EXERCISE

The feeling I get when I move my body is hard to explain, because it's something that I've lived with for so many years. Growing up, I was active so that I could compete; since I have retired, I have used exercise in a different way: for a body–mind connection that grounds me, that de-stresses me. I'm a big fan of yoga, which makes me feel wonderfully serene. I do an online class, and I actually find it quite emotional, sometimes. We need to balance all the stress and adrenaline with something like yoga that soothes the nervous system and encourages us to pay attention to our breath and what our bodies are trying to tell us. I also try to fit in three training sessions a week, which might involve using some stretch bands and dumbbells, doing some reps. It gives me a halo for the rest of the day – a glow. Sometimes it drops down to two sessions, but I don't scold myself. I just reassure myself by saying that the following week I'll do an extra session, because I know this is how I fill up my calmness cup: with movement. I also power walk with my dog, and do some mindful stretching, coupled with breathing when I have the time.

Back when I was competing, it was all about the achievement of working towards a bigger goal. And I hadn't yet experienced what it is to move, through choice alone, and to feel good in myself, because of the exercise. It was purposeful, but on a grand scale. Over the past few years, I've been redefining the purpose, and redefining and re-engaging with what exercise makes me feel as a person, as a woman, and as someone who's no longer involved in high-level sport. At first, I thought you couldn't achieve anything in 20 minutes. I thought you needed to train for at least two hours. That level of intensity was ingrained in me. And so, I had to rewrite it, adapt to what my body was telling me it needed now, and decide it was important to me and my stress levels to exercise for fun.

Mental motivation

I don't know many people who feel worse about themselves after they've exercised – they normally get a better night's sleep, too. It may be uncomfortable while doing it, and it might highlight how far you have to go on your fitness journey, but the instant dopamine hit can't be denied. Making exercise part of your routine, like brushing your teeth twice a day, is the best way to stay motivated, reduce stress and put yourself first for once, in a world where everyone else is making demands of you. Yes, your family might have to adjust their schedules and responsibilities so that you can fit it in, but it can be done. Now, how do you get motivated?

Here's how

- I realise that some people simply can't work out on their own, so finding a training buddy is a sure way to keep you engaged, whether you are in the mood or not, because letting someone else down in this process makes you feel worse.
- Treat yourself to a new outfit that makes you look and feel good – you'll be inspired to wear it.
- Have a purpose – a mantra: 'I would like to work out four times this month for 20 minutes.' Give

yourself a tick or gold star in your diary when you achieve it, and watch them mount up.

- Keep it simple. Once you accomplish your first target – keep moving it forward incrementally.
- Keep trying different sports and fitness routines until you find the one for you. I've taken up golf because I love that it gets to quench my former athlete's competitive thirst.

If working out hasn't been part of your life, you probably won't understand the purposeful energy that you get from it. Sometimes a negative experience from your school days can be enough to leave you with a negative association with exercise, or perhaps your parents never saw the value in sporting endeavour, so you were not encouraged to take part. But this is your time now. You get to start again. Exercise can be a great tool in unlocking yourself, your endorphins, and leave you feeling better about yourself. I really do believe in it: the grounding it provides, improving lung capacity, feeling that strength in your legs, which you get from walking and not being idle. We were born to move, whether you choose to hike, dance, or do interval training. And exercise builds your inner strength, too. There are a lot of demands on us daily that are found in different guises, and so you need to find that bit of strength for yourself. Strength, endurance, balance, flexibility: they're all components of everyday life.

TALKING IS SOOTHING

We all think there is some magic out there to fix everything, but those energies really do lie within you. That said, sharing and speaking with others can soothe the system, too, helping to convince you that you're on the right track, or that you deserve a break, whatever that might be. It helps to talk through your thought processes with someone you trust; a healthy dialogue creates a kind of order for your brain to contemplate. You can get clear on where you're sitting on the spectrum of emotions on any given day, and then you can begin a layering process of working out who you are, what you feel, what you're prepared to do, and what you're not prepared to do. If something is really bothering you, what are you going to do about it?

Sometimes, you don't have to share your woes; you can sit calmly with yourself for as long as you need to: sit calmly with your dilemma. It takes inner strength to decide that you're not in a position to make a decision right now and that you're not going to force it. Sometimes you have a vague understanding of what the next steps might be, but you're not emotionally ready to activate them. Accepting that is OK; it allows you peace of mind that you've acknowledged something – an emotion or a situation – for what it is, but you're giving yourself time to process it.

My gift to any woman is this: know that sometimes you are going to be swarmed by different feelings, but trust your gut, look inside yourself to a place of calm, and you will find a way. My athletics gave me a lot of tools, and invariably when you are an individual sportsman or woman, it's hard work, it's graft, it's repetition, it's positive self-talk, it's reaffirming certain emotions, but it is also giving over to the process of *doing*. Not every athlete is born confident. They will have moments of feeling confident, and moments when they don't. Certain states can be very transient, and more transient for some people than others. But when you are called upon, can you tap into those tools that can ground and calm you?

 Questions to consider when stressed

Make a note of your answers to the following:

1. What is bothering you right now?
2. Who can you discuss this with?

3. What emotions are you processing?
4. What is your emotional skill set?
5. How do you feel after a good chat with a trusted friend?

FIND PEACE AS A PARENT

As an athlete, I was taught many useful life skills, including managing frustration, managing setbacks, managing small mistakes or errors, and keeping my composure. I took most of them for granted; for example, on the occasions when I would be competing and have lactic acid building up in my calves, I would be in agony, but I would have to find the composure and mental fortitude to keep going, even if I felt as if my legs were about to drop off. For those of you who haven't ever had to suffer with this, lactic acid occurs when you're not getting enough oxygen into your body because you're using it up too quickly. You get a burning pain in the muscle tissue. It starts with the hamstrings, and it makes you feel heavy and stressed. It will start to dissipate naturally once you get more oxygenated blood back into the cells, but when you're in it, it's yucky. In those moments, my head would be screaming: *Ouch, this hurts!* But then another voice would speak up, saying: *Come on, Denise, you can do it!* However, off the field, it feels as if I've lost some of those skills, or rather, in family settings I don't always exercise those same disciplines of composure and calm.

When I find myself reacting too quickly, that's when the scales can tip a little bit. I try to find that composure when, for example, the children are asking so many things at once and it feels as if there's no time to pause for thought but I know that saying no is going to cause a big reaction. Those are the moments when I'm trying to introduce a pause and delay my response instead of reacting straight away. Sometimes, I think: *I know you're not going to be able to do that; I'm not going to take that*, or *You have to do something first*, but the way we package a *no* to our kids can be important. They can be relentless in their desires and their needs, and their immediacy of getting that *yes* from you. The *yes* is everything for them and sometimes it just can't be a *yes*. You've just got to find a way of articulating that calmly, even when you're in the middle of whatever chore you're doing or work problem you're thinking about.

When my kids are playing up, I try to maintain a level of calm, but it doesn't always work. With Troy, the youngest, I might say, 'I'm not happy when you do that. That doesn't make me feel happy when you do that.' And sometimes, I see acknowledgement or recognition that he's understood what I've said, but then sometimes he continues doing what he's doing anyway. Most often, though, he'll go a bit quiet and look at me, searching my face for proof that a fun mummy is still in there, which is always entertaining.

I try to communicate, but with children generally, including teenagers, they're not at the same intellectual and emotional levels as you are. You can impart as much of your self-control, your discipline, your annoyance as you can, and sometimes they'll get it and then sometimes they won't actually see it at all and won't be on the same page. At that point it always comes back to managing your expectations of the individual you're dealing with, and managing yourself and your feelings in that moment.

LET GO OF WORK WORRIES

It's not just with my children that I have to keep calm; it's also with work situations. Sometimes an email will come in with a request, or I'm bombarded with information, or perhaps there's something I haven't been told about, but someone is expecting something from me that hasn't yet been delivered. I can feel as if I'm in trouble when I receive that kind of email. I feel extra stress when those emails are coming in on a day when I'm not even supposed to be working. Although there's a tendency to want to respond straight away to everything all the time, I'm trying, instead, to say to myself: *I'm not actually working today.* Or, if I find I do have the time, even though I'm not supposed to be working, I might think: *Well, they've clearly forgotten that I'm not working, but I've got a window of opportunity to answer emails, so I will do that now.* But I do acknowledge the feelings I have at the time – frustration, for example – before moving forward. It's there, you can pick it out of the air. Sometimes, I might want to be left alone for a minute. Or to fire off an angry response saying, 'Have you not checked the calendar to know I'm working on something else today?' Sometimes I type out my agitation into a message, and then I don't send it. It's always best not to send agitated, angry messages, I find. And that's a top tip from me.

I would actually say the biggest and the most liberating sensation when you're dealing with stress of any kind is acknowledgement. Acknowledging that you feel pissed off with someone. Acknowledging that you feel like crap today. Acknowledging that you're not in the best mood. You don't have to label it immediately; it will come to you. But saying to yourself, or a sympathetic listener if you have one: *I'm not having a great day today, I'll be fine, I know it is not forever* really is liberating. In a moment when you're feeling overwhelmed, take a deep breath, distract yourself, do the zoom in or zoom out method I taught you in Chapter 2 on pages 86–7, and do whatever you need to in order to feel calm.

Understand what's in your on-hand toolkit at that moment, which are usually easily accessible things such as breathing, walking, taking a sip of water, whatever it might be. And then come back and recognise why it is you feel stressed or anxious or angry. Perhaps it's that you're upset by a reaction, but you don't want to allow it to fester or spiral into another 20 or 30 minutes of ranting and raving. Give it a little space, at the outset, and say to yourself: *OK, I'm annoyed by this.* Admitting it out loud might just help it to shift.

We have permission to be human and say what we really feel, and I stand my ground, at times, when I feel it would help me or the situation, but I do try to manage myself and my outbursts. I might sometimes say to people around me, or people chasing me, that I'm not having a great day, so I would appreciate it if they could limit the information they're bombarding me with. And as soon as you give clarity to your feelings and acknowledge them, and highlight it to someone else, you tend to get a better response. If everyone's in the dark nothing is going to shift – they're not mind-readers, at the end of the day. You've got to lift the veil and say: *This is what I'm thinking, this is what I'm feeling. Is it possible for you to just back off a bit?* Most people will. Most people have been there, stressed or anxious and needing to calm down a bit, and they can adapt their expectations of you in that moment to help you out.

Stop being reactive in times of stress

Make a note of your answers to the following:

1. Do you find yourself reacting quickly when someone wants something that you can't give them?
2. How can you adapt your usual way of reacting to give a calmer response?
3. How might it shift the situation positively, if you did that instead?
4. What areas of your life could you apply this to?
5. When are you going to start?

SOMEWHERE FOR YOU

A lovely way to ground yourself is to have a space you can go to when you need a moment of calm. For me, it's my living room. There's a cosy sofa, it's plush. And there's a nice cuddly throw on the sofa. There are plants in there, so there's some greenery, too. And it's quiet. It's a clean space, not clinical – there's a pop of colour in the paintings – but it's clear and clean, with a nice contrast between light and dark. I have a lovely antique glass coffee table in there, with some candles on it, which are scented and smell amazing. I go in there, put my feet up and feel as if I'm having a big hug from my own sofa, enveloped into a place of peace.

I tend to seek refuge there in the evening, once the kids are in bed, but on occasion, I'll go in in the afternoon if I need ten minutes for myself, and I just sit there quietly. I don't even put the TV on. In the evenings, it is my retreat space away from the hub of the kitchen. I have no clock in there. It is just a really different space. Kane likes to sit in with me sometimes, but there are no toys, books or racing cars. Even Steve has to play along with my rules and take his beer bottle out when he goes. My family might not like it, but they have learned to adapt. Your home is a retreat from the busyness of the world and this room of my own is where I feel most Zen.

How to create your calm space

- Allocate a calm space where you can go for some respite. Perhaps it's a dedicated room; perhaps it's one corner of a room, or it's a certain tree in your garden. You can have comfy cushions and lovely scented candles, or a snack selection.

- You get to decide who is allowed to join you in that space (if, indeed, anyone is allowed). It's *your* calm space.
- Outside your calm space, have a think about what a calm home would look and feel like for you, and if you can create it.
- Build your own feel-good playlist and have it to hand whenever you take a moment in your calm corner.

FIND INNER STRENGTH

On the following pages you'll find nine tips on finding inner strength and calm from one of the calmest people I know: my yoga teacher Nicky.

I alluded earlier to my need to actively increase calming breath-work into my life during stressful situations. Largely, these periods related to family matters, but I also went through a phase of having panic attacks, as I have explained. I knew I needed another outlet, and luckily – at that moment – I discovered Nicky. Her yoga class was recommended to me by a friend, and since my first instruction from her I knew that her teaching style was going to be a valuable part of my week, learning from her how flexibility of the body encourages flexibility of the mind. I remember tears stinging at the back of my eyes as her wisdom unlocked and opened my heart during our first encounter, and that I felt lighter and uplifted after the session, which was very powerful.

Standing in my power and grounding myself to feel calm and centred are a small part of the transferable knowledge I have obtained from introducing yoga into my daily life. I like to think that I'm a strong person and a resilient individual, but sometimes we all need a little extra help. And that's OK. Finding Nicky's yoga class was the missing piece in my self-care process, and I'm pleased to share some of her observations on stillness and authenticity, in her own words, with you here.

One: find space for yourself

I've got a monkey mind, just like many others, and I create lots of different worst-case scenarios in my head that can, and at some points have, driven me crazy. Literally. Just thinking about them makes my heart race. Yoga has helped. If I didn't have yoga, perhaps I would have found something else, perhaps drink, perhaps drugs – I don't know. But we must find that space for ourselves to reset and rebalance, whatever it is. We owe it to our calmest selves.

Two: find confidence

Yoga won't solve all your problems. But it's there. It's there for me. It's there for you. It's a safety net. I feel completely different when I'm practising yoga. I feel very confident, despite not being a confident person. Since I was a child, I've lacked an awful lot of confidence, and if you had said to me, twenty years ago, 'You're going to be a yoga teacher and stand in front of people and talk', I would have replied, 'No way!' I was very self-destructive as well when I was younger. Yoga has allowed me to feel comfortable standing in my own space; to feel stronger. See, we are not stuck. We can all change for the better if we want to.

Three: accept your limitations

The physical poses in yoga are reflections of your mind. They teach you so much about your body – your limitations and *accepting* them – and having to find comfort in the discomfort. It's very empowering. And then there's that moment when everything settles, you're in the pose. Your hips feel niggly, but you breathe through it, your feet feel a bit sore, you are stiff in the neck – and then there's that moment when you feel strong in that pose. You can take that into everyday life, because life has limits, and it can be uncomfortable, but you'll get through it.

Four: find the authentic you

Yoga teaches us to be true to ourselves. It's when we're true to ourselves, that we're the happiest. Authenticity is crucial, which is why Instagram scares me so much. The constant comparison with others that is so prevalent in the world we live in now doesn't interest me. I try to be forthright and steadfast in what I want to be. If I posted something on Instagram, every week or every month (whatever you're supposed to do), I think I would be very tempted *not* to be myself. Social media is particularly challenging for young people, and women particularly – we need to be aware of the inauthenticity of the perfection displayed there.

Five: be yourself

Be who you want to be – not who others want you to be. I'm leading my life through yoga, in the way that I want to lead it, and not focusing on what other people expect of me. I'm still the same person as when I was two, three years old, and quite busy and stressed at times, but as soon as I roll out my mat, settle and breathe, I find the peace to be myself and quieten the outside noise that makes me anxious.

Six: be self-aware

Get comfortable being on your own. I'm alone a lot, and I feel that I'm a better person when I'm on my own. Hearing myself admit that feels scary, but being on my own is my happy space. When I was younger, I wasn't happy being surrounded by so-called friends and being with a partner that was expected of me, didn't make me happy either. Now I accept that as long as all my loved ones are all right and safe, I'm happiest when I'm on my own – and we need to get comfortable admitting that. It doesn't make us lonely or antisocial, just self-aware. It makes us centred.

Seven: replenish yourself

Take care of yourself. Society drip-feeds us this notion, particularly to women, that our role is to look after everyone else before ourselves, but age and experience has taught me that you can't give to everyone else at the expense of yourself for a prolonged period of time – you need to replenish yourself, too.

Eight: trust your gut

Ask yourself questions. Listen to your answers. What do you want to do? Who do you want to be? What does a fulfilling life look like to you? You always know, don't you? My gut is always right. And my mum is usually right! I used to rebel to a certain extent, when I was younger; I used to rebel against what my mum wanted me to do. Now I know that two things I can trust are my gut and my mum. Listen to those whom you know have your best interests at heart, including yourself.

Nine: find your version of happiness

Focus on happiness. What does happiness look like to you? We might look at people on social media, or even at the school gates, and imagine that they have perfect lives, because they seem blissfully happy; but they might not be – or it might not be your version of happiness anyway. Find your own version of true happiness. You owe it to yourself.

SELF-CARE AND STILLNESS

When you encounter big adaptations, it's important to think about them in your own time. When you don't, things can spiral. With all the different things hitting us, all the different roles, and the new ways of living in this modern world – not to mention the changes happening with our kids, our parents, our partner or our work life – we must find our own space, find our own calm, because otherwise they will affect us badly.

I lost that ability for a decade in my forties. I lost that stillness. I lost that calm. My energy was all over the place, because I wanted to parent well *and* move my career forward. Space and time seemed to run away from me, and I would be up until 10.30pm every night, washing, cleaning, answering emails, until the fun part of me had just withered away and died. I needed to be more selective about how I was spending my time, but I didn't have a minute to consider what that should look like. It's hard when you have young kids or you're trying to build a career, but you've got to seek stillness. I look back now and know that I should have done things differently. Thankfully, I've been able to adapt my life to give me what I need, and that meant setting up a new system with my partner. I've had to tell Steve that I don't want a heavy, in-depth conversation first thing in the morning, because it rattles my nerves. We can talk in the afternoon, but first thing, no – I need to clear the decks and deal with everything, not get sucked into a deep discussion with him. Taking control of your head-space is essential. I try to always be on an even keel, and I always look for the positives, but I will say to him that he can't mess with my mind whenever he wants to. Being in a partnership means working out what you both want and need, at any given time.

Sometimes I wonder whether I should just lower my expectations a bit, and I might do this for a while. At other times, I have been known to go on strike; I do what the French do, and just say, 'No, this is not good enough. I'm going on strike', and I just leave everything and try to put the blinkers on. And what happens? I internalise the frustration and that mounts up, and I realise that's actually not good for me either. Nevertheless, everyone tends to step up, just for a little bit. I notice a glimmer of recognition even though it might not be at my pace, but little bits will get done.

If I'm feeling frustrated about the home – or at any other times of stress – I like to lie down and ground myself with a breathing exercise. It might be when Steve and I are on a different page and feeling out of whack, and I notice that I'm overwhelmed, taking on too much and he's not hearing me. That's when I need to pause. I need to stop the world turning for a minute and go and lie down and just rest, breathe it out. I find the foetal position very comfortable. I feel small and tucked in, comforted. I have my pillow tucked under me, on my left side. It's my safe position.

If you need to step into your own space for a bit and it's not safe to lie down, let's say you're in an office environment, walking can help, too. It doesn't have to be a long walk, but we have the elements around us for a reason. There's a reason we wash our face with cold water, a reason we go and take extra oxygen from the air outside. It's good for us, which is why we feel so amazing when we hear the sea and sink our toes in the sand. It helps us to reconnect with the inner self, the spirit. When seeing the trees, the sun and the sky, you get to leave the stress behind for a moment and feel earthed. It helps you to take control of the situation, in the moment.

I love music, too. I used music to calm my nerves the night before competing in the Olympics, and I use it now when I'm stuck in traffic. I recommend putting together a playlist of music that makes you feel happy to listen to when the stress seeps in, or even for your daily commute into work when you want to start the day on a high vibe. When I go away with my girlfriends for the weekend, we play a lot of eighties music, as that's the decade when we were at school together. We put on Suzanne Vega, and I instantly feel that I'm taking care of myself, nurturing my soul.

VALUE YOUR TIME

I really value my free time because, as a woman, there's always so much to do, isn't there? It's impossible not to have a schedule, isn't it? You can't just drift time away when you're a mum and you have to get the bulk of what needs to be done before you can allow yourself time to decompress and relax. As we have seen, I started to resent not having that ability in the evening to stop the chores or stop filling in email requests from school – or something else – to chat on the phone to a friend. What happened to that life where you could have a healthy catch-up with a mate? A woman's time seems to get lessened and pushed out, and replaced by the endless to-do list. Well, no more! I've had to consciously adapt my evenings, because in order to feel calm, I need time to talk with my friends.

 Look differently at your time

Make a note of your answers to the following:

1. How would you like to spend your evenings?
2. Do you get time to be with friends?
3. What boundaries do you have around cooking, mealtimes and family?
4. What could you let slip, if it meant that you can do something more enjoyable?
5. What's the most relentless aspect of running a home that makes you feel resentful?

As my children get older, I've increasingly noticed that my own needs have been sidelined, and part of that is my fault. I have adapted *too much* into the role of wife and mother. Now, in my early fifties, I need to be re-engaging with what I need in order to feel good while being there for my loved ones. We women need to be the ultimate chameleons – we wake up, there's always a wash to put on, there's always something to do and someone who needs us – but we really do need to push back on the limitations this brings us, because the demands are relentless. There's this expectation that we will shoulder all the work and still be cheerful, happy, an amazing sex goddess, and all the rest. No. No. No. Sometimes we are freaking tired and overwhelmed, we need to restore our inner peace and calm, and you know what? Everyone else can adapt to us for a bit, so we can adapt back into being the serene powerhouse they know we can be.

Five ways to build inner strength and calm

1. Focus on the positive and feel optimistic about the future.
2. During periods of stress, talk it out with people who have your back.

3. Have a calm space to sit in silence, meditate or listen to calming music.

4. Roll into the foetal position, if you need to feel safe and comforted.

5. Remember that your time should be valued and that you deserve time to rest and play just like everyone else in your home or in your workplace.

Conclusion

Can you be fearless when it comes to making decisions about your life? Can you minimise the duration of the free fall when someone or something unexpectedly presents a situation that you didn't expect? I hope that this book offers you an opportunity to reflect and acts as a reminder that only you have the power to direct the changes you want to see, whether you need to do this by reaching out, digging deep or letting go.

You will experience setbacks, failures and crushing lows, and you will feel utterly overwhelmed at times. We all do; you are never alone in that. In those moments it's like being in the heptathlon when an event has gone horribly wrong, you sit in that moment, accept, and make the mental adjustment so that the emotion does not impact the next several events. Your focus is to rebuild yourself and get back on the horse. You use adaptability to get back into the race.

Some of the most heart-warming comments I receive are from people who have chosen to use the Couch to 5k app to start their running journey and have selected me as their coach. They tend to thank me for helping them, but actually they have helped themselves by recognising that they need to do something different in their lives. They know that it's going to be uncomfortable, but step by step (literally) they are demonstrating their own inner strength, and I love that. You don't have to be an Olympian to do that – you just have to try.

I feel very blessed and believe that my successes have come from a consistency in behaviour, using positive thinking and embracing new challenges both big and small. I forgive myself for mistakes but I keep the labels that I *choose* to wear about myself. I advocate embracing change as an opportunity to learn and develop, because it's something that I wholeheartedly believe in myself. Stepping away from my pundit role with BBC Sport wasn't easy, and not something that I initially wanted to do, so at first I resisted the ultimatum placed at my door; however, with careful soul searching and deliberation I will now step back into the role of President of UK Athletics, fully accepting that I am moving to where I'm supposed to be. Evolving and journeying to new pastures is always a little daunting and will no doubt be challenging. Isn't this how we know that we are truly living and not simply existing?

Be open to change. Adapt your own ideas about what you're capable of and what you can be. I remember being invited by then Prime Minister David Cameron to fly to Washington to attend a state dinner as part of a British contingent just before the London Olympics with a load of other Brits; so there I was, hovering around with Richard Branson, Idris Elba and Damian Lewis – me, Denise Lewis, with these legends. We sat down for dinner, then John Legend played, and after dessert and coffee, we were introduced to the US President and First Lady: Barack and Michelle Obama. My head was buzzing with the same excited phrase: *I can't believe this is happening. Is this really happening? I can't believe this is happening.* Then my name was announced, I walked up and I shook Barack's hand, shook Michelle's hand, and I was drinking in these people who were such symbols of change. Our meeting was brief, we had perhaps ten seconds before the next person's name was announced, but it was a seismic moment for me, and a lesson for us all: don't let the unknown intimidate you into standing still.

There have been various moments like that since then, and it makes me think each time: *I'm clearly meant to be in this position. I'm not sure how or why, but I am.* We must keep learning, keep doing, keep changing, keep growing.

When you live in a world of competing demands, as all women do these days, it is the ability to adapt that will allow us to find calm in the madness. We need self-belief to keep going despite the unexpected twists and turns, and the courage to face new situations head-on, refusing to live in denial or buried under anxiety.

We all need to have our own definition of what success looks like. I ask you to remember that you are multifaceted and capable of so much in all areas of your life. If you can find a winning formula in one aspect of your life, can you do it elsewhere? In this way, you will be incrementally progressing, and that will feel good; it will shine out and radiate from you when people meet you.

I started athletics because I was curious as to how good I could be, and that curiosity for life has never left me. It's what drives our children to develop and for technology to evolve. This curiosity circles back to us and our ability to adapt to all that this wonderful, scary, beautiful and competitive world throws at us. I feel that I've done this, and I've won a gold. I hope this book has unlocked that drive in you, too.

Now, go get it!

Denise

Acknowledgements

I'd like to take this opportunity to thank the many women who have influenced me, guided me, laughed with me, supported me emotionally, boosted my confidence and allowed me to reciprocate. This journey would be pretty dull without you.

A special mention to K. M. Zouhary who walked into my life by chance at an Estée Lauder dinner and shone a light into my soul when I needed reminding about the power of individuality and female leadership.